Legal Aspects of Patient Confidentiality

BJN monograph

Legal Aspects of Health Care series

Bridgit Dimond

Quay Books

Mark Allen
Publishing Ltd

w 32

Quay Books Division, Mark Allen Publishing Limited,
Jesses Farm, Snow Hill, Dinton, Wiltshire, SP3 5HN

British Library Cataloguing-in-Publication Data
A catalogue record is available for this book

© Bridgit Dimond 2002
ISBN 1 85642 202X

Printed in the UK by Cromwell Press, Trowbridge, Wiltshire

Contents

Acknowledgements

I would like to give my special thanks to Dr Yardley who read the entire typescript and made some valuable suggestions to the text and also recommended that the book should be marketed to other health professionals as well as nurses, since the issues considered here are important to them all. I should also record my considerable debt to Bette Griffiths in proof reading the book, providing the index and her constant encouragement and support.

Bridgit Dimond
October, 2001

Preface

This monograph follows the publication of a series of articles in the *British Journal of Nursing* on confidentiality. The need for a book for health professionals setting out the law and practice on confidentiality led to Quay Books agreeing that the articles, updated and revised, could form the basis of a concise publication covering the main concerns which arise in respecting the duty of confidentiality. It is hoped that all registered health professionals (in the book referred to as practitioners for convenience) will find the book of value in their professional work, which involves the protection of the rights of the patient and working within the confines of the law. Trust is at the heart of the health professional/patient relationship, yet many practitioners find themselves in situations where they are torn between their duty of confidentiality to the patient and other duties. Knowledge of the law should assist them in resolving such dilemmas.

1

The duty to respect patient confidentiality

Box 1.1: Breach of confidentiality

Staff nurse (S/N) Brown discovers that a recent admission on the surgical ward is a member of a famous pop band. On a promise of total secrecy, she tells her friend that he has been admitted and will be having an operation for a hernia repair the following day. To her embarrassment and shame, the next day the papers publish the story and the disclosure was eventually traced to S/N Brown. What legal repercussions are likely and why?

The duty to respect patient confidentiality arises from a variety of sources including the duty of care to the patient, the contract of employment, professional codes of practice and Acts of Parliament.

Duty of care to the patient

Implicit within the duty of care owed to the patient is the duty to recognise the right of the patient to have personal information kept confidential (*Furniss* v. *Fitchett* [1958]). In theory, the pop singer in the case scenario (*Box 1.1*) could sue the employers of the nurse for their vicarious liability for the breach of confidentiality by the nurse. However, he is unlikely to do this since more publicity would be generated, when clearly he wished the admission to be kept secret. He would have to show that he suffered harm as a result of the disclosure if he were to rely upon an action for breach of the duty of care. When royalty and other famous persons are admitted to hospital, their public relations officers agree with the hospital on an announcement of the admission and on condition bulletins which are made during their stay. If, however, they wish for the admission and condition to be kept confidential, then this is their right. Had he been aware of the intent to publish before it actually took place, then he could have sought an injunction from the court to prevent the publication going ahead. An injunction is an order of the court prohibiting specified action taking place. Failure to comply with an injunction could lead to imprisonment for contempt of court. In the scenario the example of a pop singer is used but, of course, the right to confidentiality applies to all patients, not just the famous.

Duty under the contract of employment

Staff Nurse Brown could face disciplinary proceedings. It is either an express term (ie. set out in writing or mentioned by word of mouth) of her contract of employment or an implied term (ie. a term recognised by the courts as implicit within the contract of employment) that she should respect the confidential nature of information about patients. By failing to comply with this term of the contract of employment, she could be disciplined, the ultimate sanction being the loss of her job. Should she consider this to be an unfair dismissal, if she has the requisite continuous service, she could apply to the employment tribunal for a hearing. The employers would have to show the reason for the dismissal and the tribunal would decide if the employers acted reasonably in relying upon this reason to justify dismissal.

Duty of confidentiality arising from professional codes of practice

The UKCC (and after April 2002 the Nursing and Midwifery Council [NMC]), the Council for Professions Supplementary to Medicine (after April 2002 the Health Professions Council [HPC]) and the GMC require all their registered practitioners to recognise the duty of confidentiality owed to the patient as part of their *Codes of Professional Conduct* (UKCC, 1992). Clause 10 of the UKCC Code sets out the duty of confidentiality:

As a registered nurse... you... must: protect all confidential information concerning patients and clients obtained in the course of professional practice and make disclosures only with consent, when required by the order of a court or where you can justify disclosure in the public interest.

This duty is further expanded in the *Guidelines for Professional Practice* (UKCC, 1996) which emphasise that:

Confidentiality should only be broken in exceptional circumstances and should only occur after careful consideration that you can justify your action.

Whether or not S/N Brown loses her job, she could face professional conduct hearings before the UKCC for her breach of the Code. It is likely that on the facts the UKCC would consider disclosure of confidential information about a patient, without any lawful justification, to be misconduct by a nurse. It has various sanctions, the ultimate being removal from the register. If this is the outcome, the nurse would lose her job. Other health professionals such as psychologists also have codes of conduct which require members to recognise the duty of confidentiality and breach of this duty in circumstances where not justified could result in disciplinary action.

Duties arising from statutory provisions

Sometimes Acts of Parliament lay down clear provisions in relation to confidentiality and make breach of a duty of confidentiality a criminal offence. Thus, the Human Fertilisation and Embryology Act 1990 (as amended by the 1992 Act) makes stringent provisions on disclosure of information (see *Chapter 6*). Other statutes and regulations with penalties for breach of confidentiality include:

- Abortion Regulations 1991 made under the Abortion Act 1967
- NHS (Venereal Disease) Regulations 1974
- The Data Protection Act 1998.

None of these apply in S/N Brown's case. They are considered in later chapters of this book.

Human Rights Act 1998

The provisions of this Act came into force in England and Wales on 2 October, 2000 (Dimond, 1999; Dimond, 2000). They came into force on devolution in Scotland. The Act required all public authorities or organisations carrying out functions of a public nature to respect the European Convention of Human Rights which is set out in Schedule 1 to the Act. In addition, it gave a right for citizens to bring an action in the courts of the UK if they considered that their human rights as set out in the Schedule had been breached by a public authority. Judges were also required to refer back to Parliament any legislation which they considered to be incompatible with the Articles set out in the European Convention of Human Rights. One of the most significant changes brought about by this Act, is that people no longer have to take their case to Strasbourg for a hearing before the European Courts of Human Rights but can avoid the additional cost and delay and bring the case in local courts. If a judicial review is sought of a decision which is considered to be in breach of the human rights recognised in the Convention, then legal aid is available for this action.

Article 8 of the Convention:

1. Everyone has the right to respect for his private and family life, his home and his correspondence.
2. There shall be no interference by a public authority with the exercise of this right except such as is in accordance with the law and is necessary in a democratic society in the interests of national security, public safety or the economic well-being of the country, for the prevention of disorder or crime, for the protection of health or morals, or for the protection of the rights and freedoms of others.

Paragraph 2 shows that the right to respect for private and family life is not absolute but qualified. Circumstances are specified where the Article might not apply. The European Court has recognised the importance of preserving the confidentiality of medical records (*Z.* v. *Finland* [1998]). The European Court of Human Rights decided that the refusal of the UK to amend its system of registering births so as to permit post-operative transexuals to record their new sexual identity was not a breach of Article 8 (*Sheffield* v. *UK* [1999]). Article 8 also has to be read in conjunction with Article 10 which recognises a right to freedom of expression. Like Article 8, this right is also qualified and if there were a conflict between one person's right to freedom of expression and another person's right to privacy, a judge would have to determine how those respective rights should be respected and the merits of each case. For example, a person may consider that a press account of their private life infringed their right to privacy. However, if that person was prominent in public life, proclaiming family values, yet supporting a mistress, the press may consider that freedom of expression was justified to expose such hypocrisy.

It is not clear how much additional protection this Article adds to the duty of confidentiality in health care, but clearly privacy is a wider concept than confidentiality. For example, on a ward round a consultant might draw the curtains around a bed and then discuss the patient's diagnosis and treatment, talking in confidence to the multidisciplinary team, and attempting to respect the principles of confidentiality. If that conversation could be heard by others in the ward, it could be said that in practice there was a breach of confidentiality. In contrast, if a journalist saw a famous person being admitted to a psychiatric hospital and published an article on this, there would be no breach of confidentiality since that information had not been obtained through any confidential disclosures. However, the publication would probably be a breach of Article 8 and the person's respect for privacy unless publication could be justified under Article 10 as part of the right of free expression.

Access and human rights

Patients may be able to use certain Articles of the European Convention of Human Rights to justify their obtaining access to their records. This issue is considered in *Chapter 3*.

Duty as part of the trust obligation between health professional and patient

The law recognises that there is a trust obligation between the health professional and the patient. If there were to be a disclosure, the patient would have a remedy for this breach of confidentiality. The pop singer could complain to the NHS trust on this basis. S/N Brown has failed to respect the trust which she took on as a nurse.

Breach of trust by S/N Brown's friend

S/N Brown could claim that her friend failed to respect the confidentiality of the information which she had (wrongly) disclosed to her. This is actionable. In the case of *Stephens* v. *Avery and others* [1988] (*Box 1.2,* overleaf), the claimant succeeded for breach of trust. In practice, of course, it is unlikely that S/N Brown would sue her friend. First, a basic principle in legal disputes is never sue any person who is unlikely to be able to pay the compensation demanded and, second, even if her friend obtained payment from the newspaper for passing on that information and therefore had funds to pay compensation, it is unlikely that the court would make an award which would result in the person guilty of the original disclosure benefiting from the profits of that disclosure.

Remedies for enforcing the duty of confidentiality

If a person fears that information which has been disclosed in confidence is likely to be passed on to others, then an application can be made to the courts for an injunction to prevent the publication or disclosure of that information. Clearly the advantage of this action is that it prevents the disclosure. Other remedies are available after the unjustified disclosure takes place, including an action for compensation for breach of contract if the duty of confidentiality is contained in a contract, or an action in the tort of negligence for compensation for harm which has occurred. Mental harm would have to amount to a significant mental illness for compensation to be payable. The court also has power to issue a declaration as to the rights of the claimant. Where the claim is brought under the Human Rights Act, then a declaration can be made that the disclosure is in breach of a specified Article and the court can award compensation.

Box 1.2: *Stephens* v. *Avery* **and others [1988]**

Unconscionable disclosure
The plaintiff and first defendant were close friends who freely discussed matters of a personal and private nature on the express basis that what the plaintiff told the first defendant was secret and disclosed in confidence. The first defendant passed on to the second and third defendants, who were the editor and publisher of a newspaper, details of the plaintiff's lesbian relationship with a woman who had been killed by her husband. The plaintiff brought an action against the defendants, claiming damages on the grounds that the information was confidential and was knowingly published by the newspaper in breach of the duty of confidence owed by the first defendant to the plaintiff. In an action by the defendants to strike out the claim since it showed no reasonable cause of action, the defendants failed and appealed to the Chancery Division. They lost on the grounds that, although the courts would not enforce a duty of confidence relating to matters which had a grossly immoral tendency, information relating to sexual conduct could be the subject of a legally enforceable duty of confidence if it would be unconscionable for a person, who had received information on the express basis that it was confidential, subsequently to reveal that information to another.

Conclusion

The duty of confidentiality is clear with the various sources of this duty acting in parallel. Any case of unauthorised disclosure and breach of confidentiality could give rise to different proceedings all considering different aspects of the situation, such as: employment duties, professional duties, criminal offences. The rights set out in the European Convention relating to a right to respect for privacy and family life may increase the number of cases where it is argued that there has been a failure to respect the duty of confidentiality. This may widen the basis of claims. What is often confusing to the practitioner is understanding the circumstances when disclosure may be justified, and it is to this difficult area that we turn in subsequent chapters.

References

Dimond B (1999) *Patients' Rights, Responsibilities and the Nurse*. 2nd edn. Quay Books division, Mark Allen Publishing Limited, Dinton, Salisbury, Wiltshire

Dimond B (2001) *The Legal Aspects of Nursing*. 3rd edn. Pearson Education, Harlow, Essex

Furniss v. *Fitchett* [1958] NZLR 396

Sheffield v. *UK* [1999] 27 EHRR 163

Stephens v. *Avery and others* [1988] 2 All ER 477

United Kingdom Central Council for Nursing, Midwifery and Health Visiting (1992) *Code of Professional Conduct for the Nurse, Midwife and Health Visitor*. UKCC, London

United Kingdom Central Council for Nursing, Midwifery and Health Visiting (1996) *Guidelines for Professional Practice*. UKCC, London

Z. v. *Finland* [1998] 25 EHRR 371

2

Disclosure of information in the public interest

Box 2.1: Case scenario

Staff nurse (S/N) Black was a district nurse in a deprived inner city area. While visiting one family she realised that piled up in the corner of the living room were boxes of video recorders. She commented on them to the patient who became flushed and said that her husband was a trader and brought some of the stock home. S/N Black was convinced that they were stolen goods and decided that it was her duty as a good citizen to report this to the police. What is the law?

In the first chapter the sources of the duty of confidentiality were considered and it was noted that the health professional is bound to recognise the duty to protect all confidential information about the patient. This duty is subject to specific exceptions. These exceptions include the following:

- disclosure with the consent of the patient
- disclosure in the best interests of the patient (eg. between members of the multidisciplinary team caring for the patient. This raises additional issues as to who belongs to the multidisciplinary team)
- disclosure as required by the court (*Chapter 4*)
- disclosure as required by statute (*Chapters 5, 7, 10, 11* and *14*)
- disclosure in the public interest.

This chapter discusses one of the most difficult exceptions to the duty of confidentiality: that of disclosure in the public interest.

In its guidelines for professional practice (UKCC, 1996), the UKCC explains the exception relating to the public interest. Its definition of public interest is the:

Interests of an individual, or groups of individuals or of society as a whole, and would, for example, cover matters such as serious crime, child abuse, drug trafficking or other activities which place others at serious risk.

The UKCC advises the practitioner to discuss the matter fully with other professional colleagues and, if appropriate, consult the UKCC or a membership organisation. Having made the decision, it is essential that the practitioner writes down the reasons for the disclosure as:

You then have written justification for the action which you took if this becomes necessary and you can also review the decision later in the light of future developments.

Child abuse

There is no dispute that disclosure in the public interest must include protecting children. If it comes to the notice of a practitioner that a child is being or is likely to be abused, whether physically, sexually or emotionally, then there would be a duty to report this to the appropriate person or organisation. This would be the person identified within the area child protection procedures. The procedures suggested by the UKCC should be followed and the fact of and justification for the disclosure carefully recorded (see also *Chapters 10* and *15*).

Serious harm to another person

If there is a reasonable fear that a person could cause physical harm to another, then this would probably be a justification for disclosure in the public interest. This was the subject of a dispute in a decided case where a psychiatric patient argued that the report of a medical examination which he had requested from an independent psychiatrist should not have been disclosed to others (see the case of *W*. v. *Egdell*, *Box 2.2*)

The ruling of the Court of Appeal in this case could apply to situations where a person discloses information to a practitioner which indicates that others are at serious risk from that patient. Such a reasonable belief would justify the practitioner in seeking to discuss this with senior managers and professional colleagues and in taking the appropriate action. The principle of disclosure in the public interest to prevent serious harm to others would also apply to situations of infectious disease, which would come under the notifiable diseases legislation (see *Chapter 5*).

Box 2.2: *W*. v. *Egdell* [1989]

'W.' was detained in a secure hospital under section 37/41 of the Mental Health Act 1983 following a conviction for manslaughter on the grounds of diminished responsibility. He had shot dead five people and two others required major surgery. He applied to a Mental Health Review Tribunal for discharge or transfer to a regional secure unit with a view to his eventual discharge. His responsible medical officer supported his application but it was opposed by the Secretary of State. W. obtained an independent medical report from Dr Egdell who strongly opposed his transfer. In the light of this report W. withdrew the application to the tribunal.

Dr Egdell had assumed that this report would be made available to the hospital and the tribunal. He sought the permission of W. to place his report before the hospital but was refused permission. Dr Egdell then sent the report to the managers asking them to forward a copy to the Home Secretary since he considered that his examination had cast new light on the dangerousness of W. and it ought to be known to those responsible for his care and for the formulation of any recommendations for discharge.

Subsequently, the Home Secretary referred W. to a Mental Health Review Tribunal. The Home Secretary sent a copy of Dr Egdell's report to the tribunal. W. then issued writs against Dr Egdell, the hospital board, the Home Secretary and the Secretary of State for Health and the tribunal, seeking injunctions preventing the defendants from using this material and claiming damages for breach of confidentiality. The trial judge held that the court had to balance the interest to be served by non-disclosure against the interest served by disclosure. Since W. was not an ordinary member of the public but a detained patient in a secure unit, the safety of the public should be the main criterion. Dr Egdell had a duty to the public to place the result of his examination before the proper authorities if, in his opinion, the public interest so required. The public interest in disclosure outweighed W.'s private interest.

The Court of Appeal supported this reasoning and stated:

A consultant psychiatrist who becomes aware, even in the course of a confidential relationship, of information which leads him, in the exercise of what the court considers a sound professional judgement, to fear that such decisions may be made on inadequate information and with a real risk of consequent danger to the public, is entitled to take such steps as are reasonable in the circumstances to communicate the grounds of his concern to the responsible authorities.

Lord Justice Bingham

Serious harm to the patient

What if a patient discloses that following a diagnosis of terminal illness he does not wish to continue to live but will end his life? While to attempt suicide is no longer a crime since the Suicide Act 1961, it is a crime to aid and abet another person to attempt to commit suicide. In a recent case a woman terminally ill with motor neurone disease lost her attempt to obtain a declaration from the court that it would be lawful for her husband to end her life so that she could die with dignity (*R. (Pretty)* v. *DPP* [2001]; this case is further discussed in *Chapters 3* and *12*).

It may be that the patient is profoundly depressed and could, with appropriate counselling and assistance, enjoy a good standard of life for his remaining time. There would, therefore, appear to be clear justification for the practitioner to notify other professional persons who could offer the patient some assistance. Ideally, the practitioner should attempt to obtain the patient's consent to this disclosure so that there is no breach of confidentiality (see *Chapter 12*). If the patient does not consent to the disclosure, passing on this information to others may be justified as being in the public interest to prevent serious harm to the patient.

Serious criminal act

With regard to S/N Black in the case scenario (*Box 2.1*): are the circumstances which she faces sufficiently serious to justify disclosure in the public interest and do they place others at serious risk? There is no Act of Parliament which requires citizens to report their suspicions that a criminal act has been or is being committed, with the exception of acts of terrorism. The Prevention of Terrorism Acts (annually agreed) does require people to notify the police if they suspect activities relating to terrorism. Road traffic legislation requires the reporting of a road accident involving personal injuries or death. However, these are the only statutory requirements in relation to reporting crimes.

Practitioners should not see their role as police informants. They should, of course, take appropriate action with suspected child abuse or other circumstances where there is a serious risk of personal injury. The situation which S/N Black encounters does not come within this category and therefore it does not come within the UKCC's definition of public interest.

Benefit fraud

Similar difficulties of interpreting the 'public interest' exist in disclosure about benefit fraud. If a practitioner becomes aware that a family or individual is defrauding social security should this be reported? The Government is appealing to individuals to notify agencies of evidence of such criminal behaviour. However, it is suggested that the practitioner's prime duty is to provide health care for the patient, and unless serious harm to a person is likely, then there is no justification for disclosure. It is always possible for legislation to be enacted which makes it a criminal offence to fail to make known reasonable suspicions of criminal conduct, including fraud, which would radically change the role of the health professional. Such proposed legislation would probably be rigorously challenged by many health professionals.

Conclusion

The conclusion must be that S/N Black is in breach of her duty of confidentiality to the patient and the disclosure is not justified in the public interest. In theory, the family could complain to her employers. If a prosecution ensues, S/N Black could be called upon to give evidence. If she had decided not to inform the police, but the family were prosecuted anyway, she could still be called upon to give evidence in court. (This is considered in *Chapter 4*.)

Provisions relating to disclosure are contained in the Data Protection Act 1998 and it is to this we turn in the next chapter.

References

R. (Pretty) v. *Director of Public Prosecutions, Secretary of State for the Home Department Intervening.* Times Law Report, 5 December 2001 HL

United Kingdom Central Council for Nursing, Midwifery and Health Visiting (1996) *Guidelines for Professional Practice*. UKCC, London

W. v. *Egdell* [1989] 1 All ER 1089, *The Times*, 20 November 1989 Court of Appeal

3

Statutory provisions

Data Protection Act 1998; Freedom of Information Act 2000; and Health and Social Care Act 2001

Box 3.1: Case scenario

Assistant director of patient services, Ron Grey RGN, was the liaison officer with a computer firm for the automated processing of all patient records. He was asked to explain to a group of nurses the significance of the Data Protection Act 1998 and the legal requirements in respect of access to and use of the computerised records.

Until the passing of the Data Protection Act 1998 there had been a clear distinction between the legal requirements relating to computerised patient records and records in manual form. The former came under the rules of the Data Protection Act 1984 and the latter under the Access to Health Records Act 1990. However, the 1998 Act applies to patient records whether they are held in a manual form or computerised form. The Access to Health Records Act 1998 has been repealed except in the provisions relating to the records of those who have died (see below). The 1998 Act resulted from the European Directive (95/46/EC) which was designed to give further protection to individuals on the processing of personal data and on the free movement of such data. The Department of Health has provided advice and guidance on the legislation (Department of Health HSC 2000/009, see *Appendix I*). The Information Commissioner has also provided legal guidance (Information Commissioner, Legal Guidance).

The 1998 Act slightly amends the data protection principles (*Table 3.1*). The principles are further explained in Part 2 of Schedule 1. The 1998 Act has several Schedules. Schedules 1, 2 and 3 relate to the basic principles and the processing of personal data, eg. contractual purposes; compliance with a legal obligation; protection of the vital interests of the data subject; the administration of justice; the exercise of functions of the Crown or government department or other functions of a public nature; or meeting the legitimate interests of the data controller or a third party. These Schedules are included as appendices to the Department of Health circular.

Records relating to physical or mental health come within the definition of sensitive personal data. One of Schedule 3 conditions must be satisfied. These conditions include:

a. The explicit consent of the data subject
b. The use of the data is necessary to protect the vital interests of the data subject of another person and consent cannot be given by or on behalf of the data subject. (This situation would obviously cover records relating to the mentally incapacitated adult and children.)
c. The use of the data is necessary for medical purposes (including the purposes of preventive medicine, medical diagnosis, medical research, the provision of care and treatment and the management of healthcare services) and is undertaken by a health professional or a person who owes a duty of confidentiality which is equivalent to that which would arise if that person were a health professional.

Some of the terms used in the Data Protection Act 1998 are given different definitions from those used in the 1984 Act, for example:

❖ The data subject has the same meaning as under the 1984 Act, ie. 'the individual who is the subject of personal data'.

Table 3.1: Data protection principles 1998

1. Personal data shall be processed fairly and lawfully and, in particular, shall not be processed unless:

   a. at least one of the conditions in Schedule 2 is met; and

   b. in the case of sensitive personal data, at lease one of the conditions in Schedule 3 is also met

2. Personal data shall be obtained only for one or more specified and lawful purpose, and shall not be further processed in any manner incompatible with that purpose or those purposes

3. Personal data shall be adequate, relevant and not excessive in relation to the purpose or purposes for which they are processed

4. Personal data shall be accurate and, where necessary, kept up-to-date

5. Personal data processed for any purpose or purposes shall not be kept for longer than is necessary for that purpose(s)

6. Personal data shall be processed in accordance with the rights of data subjects under the 1998 Act

7. Appropriate technical and organisational measures shall be taken against unauthorised or unlawful processing of personal data and against accidental loss or destruction of, or damage to, personal data

8. Personal data shall not be transferred to a country or territory outside the European economic area unless that country or territory ensures an adequate level of protection for the rights and freedoms of data subjects in relation to the processing of personal data

❖ The data protection registrar, who is the national officer responsible for the oversight of the implementation of the law, is now to be known as the commissioner.

❖ The data controller (formerly known as the data user) is the person who determines the purposes for which and the manner in which any personal data are to be processed.

❖ Data now includes manually held records if they form part of a relevant filing system. This means that the set is structured by reference to individuals so that specific information relating to a particular individual is readily accessible. How this is interpreted in relation to hospital or community manual records will depend on court cases. It is probably best practice if, pending any court case on its meaning, medical records officers work on the basis that the data protection principles should apply to all patient records in whatever format they are held.

The rights of the individual under the 1998 Act are shown in *Table 3.2*. Section 30 enables the Secretary of State to draw up specific provisions relating to personal data of physical or mental health or condition of the data subject. The Secretary of State can exempt such data from subject information provisions. This is similar to the 1984 Act and the statutory instrument relating to access to health records. The statutory instrument for the 1998 Act is explained in *Appendix II* (taken from the Department of Health Circular HSC 2000/009). Access is excluded if serious harm to the physical or mental health or condition of the applicant or another person could be reasonably foreseen.

Information Commissioner

The Information Commissioner has taken on the role of the Data Protection Commissioner and has the responsibility for promoting good practice and observance of the laws, for providing an information service and for encouraging the development of codes of practice. The Commissioner has considerable powers of enforcement under Part 3 and 5 of the Act. These include the power to serve enforcement notices and notices of entry and inspection. Offences under the Act are:

- Offences relating to failure to notify the commissioner or comply with his requests

- Unlawfully obtaining personal data
- Unlawful selling of personal data
- Forcing a person to compel access
- Unlawful disclosure of information by the commissioner/staff or agent.

Table 3.2: Rights of the data subject under the Data Protection Act 1998
1.   Right of subject access (sections 7–9)
2.   Right to prevent processing likely to cause damage or distress (section 10)
3.   Right to prevent processing for direct marketing purposes (section 11)
4.   Right in relation to automated decision taking (section 12)
5.   Right to take action for compensation if the individual suffers damage by any contravention of the Act by the data controller (section 13)
6.   Right to take action to rectify, block, erase or destroy inaccurate data (section 14)
7.   Right to make a request to the commissioner for an assessment to be made as to whether any provision of the Act has been contravened (section 42)

Case scenario

What specific advice can be given to Ron in the case scenario? First, in preparation for his role, Ron must write to the information commissioner for an explanatory guide to the legislation.[1] He could then discuss with the officer designated as data controller within his organisation the details of the registration under the Act, and the

1   Information Commissioner (Registrar), Wycliffe House, Water Lane, Wilmslow, Cheshire SK9 5AF. Information line: 01625 545745

process by which the records are to be placed on computer and a code of practice for ensuring that the data protection principles are followed in the organisation. He will agree with the computer firm and the senior management levels of access and passwords so that unauthorised persons cannot gain access to the records. He will also ensure that records which are not to be placed on the computer, but will continue to be manually held, will be subject to the same restrictions of access.

He will ensure that staff attend training sessions both on how to use the computerised system and on understanding the principles of the Data Protection Act. They need to know that it is a criminal offence to breach these principles and that they have a clear duty to protect patient confidentiality and prevent unauthorised access. He will also make contact with the NHS board member who is designated as the Caldicott guardian (see *Chapter 8*) and who has responsibilities for the security of information across the trust.

Ron will have to ensure that he keeps up-to-date with information from the Information Commissioner and with advice provided by the Department of Health. He must take steps to provide ongoing revision training and to ensure that registered practitioners understand that, like health and safety rules, confidentiality is not a subject which can be left to a single officer within the organisation. Each individual has a personal and professional responsibility to ensure that the law is implemented and that patients' rights are protected.

Access to records of dead patients

The only provisions of the Access to Health Records Act 1990 still valid are those applying to the records of dead patients. Section 3 (as amended by the Data Protection Act 1998, Schedule 16, Part 1) enables a personal representative of the patient or any person who may have a claim arising out of the patient's death to apply for access to the deceased's health records.

Personnel records

Under Data Protection legislation, employees also have the right to access their personnel files, whether they are in computerised format or held in manual files. A code of practice has been issued by the Information Commissioner on the use of personal data by employers which provides advice on the use of data in recruitment, references, appraisal, sickness records, medical and drug tests, email monitoring and phone use.

Access to Medical Reports Act 1988

This Act came into force on 1 January, 1989. It gives an individual a right of access to any medical report relating to himself which has been supplied by a medical practitioner for employment or insurance purposes. Before any such medical report can be supplied, the individual must be notified that it is being requested and give his consent. The medical practitioner must not supply the report unless he has the consent of the individual. He is also required to give the individual the opportunity of access to it and to be allowed to correct any errors. These provisions apply unless twenty-one days have elapsed since notifying the individual of the intention to provide a report. The medical report must be retained by the medical practitioner for at least six months from the date on which it was supplied.

There is an exemption from individual access where the medical practitioner is of the opinion that disclosure would be likely to cause serious harm to the physical or mental health of the individual, or would indicate the intentions of the practitioner in respect of the individual or where the identity of another person would be made known.

Access to health records and the articles of the European Convention

In addition to rights under the Data Protection Act access provisions, a patient may be able to claim that Article 8 (see *Chapter 1*) entitles them to have access to their health records. In one case (*R.* v. *Mid Glamorgan FHSA ex parte Martin* [1995]) the Court of Appeal held that the patient did not have an absolute right to access records which had been created before the Access to Health Records came into force and that there had been no breach of Article 8 of the European Convention of Human Rights. The doctor, however, had a duty to act in the best interests of the patient in deciding upon disclosure. In another case where the applicant was seeking access to his social services files (*Gaskin* v. *United Kingdom* (1989)) the European Court of Human Rights held that Article 8 had been breached because there was no system for independently reviewing whether access should be granted.

Health and Social Care Act 2001

Section 60 of the Health and Social Care Act 2001 gives the Secretary of State powers to make, by regulations, provision for regulating the processing of prescribed patient information for medical purposes as he considers necessary or expedient:

   a. in the interests of improving patient care, or
   b. in the public interest.

The Regulations may make provision:

   a. for requiring prescribed communications of any nature which contain patient information to be disclosed by health service bodies in prescribed circumstances:

       i. to the person to whom the information relates

      ii. (where it relates to more than one person) to the person to whom it principally relates, or

     iii. to a prescribed person on behalf of any such person as is mentioned in sub-paragraph i. or ii.

b. for requiring or authorising the disclosure or other processing of prescribed patient information to or by persons of any prescribed description subject to compliance with any prescribed conditions (including conditions requiring prescribed undertakings to be obtained from such persons as to the processing of such information)

c. for securing, that, where prescribed patient information is processed by a person in accordance with the regulations, anything done by him in so processing the information shall be taken to be lawfully done despite any obligation of confidence owed by him in respect of it

d. for creating offences punishable on summary conviction by a fine not exceeding level 5 on the standard scale or such other level as is prescribed or for creating other procedures for enforcing any provisions of the regulations.

Section 60 (3)–(7) place restrictions on the Regulations which can be made.

In spite of these limitations on the power to make regulations, these are extremely extensive powers given to the Secretary of State and much will depend upon the conditions which are laid down in the regulations. At the time of writing the Regulations are awaited.

For the purposes of section 60, patient information is defined as:

a. information (however recorded) which relates to the physical or mental health or condition of an individual, to the diagnosis of this condition or to his care or treatment, and

    b. information (however recorded) which is to any extent derived directly or indirectly, from such information.

Such information is confidential if,

    a. the identity of the individual in question is ascertainable from that information or from that information and other information which is in the possession of, or is likely to come into the possession of, the person processing that information, and

    b. that information was obtained or generated by a person who, in the circumstances, owed an obligation of confidence to that individual.

Medical purpose is defined to include preventative medicine, diagnosis, research, provision of care and treatment, the management of health and social care services and informing patients about diagnosis, treatment and care.

Processing means the use, disclosure or obtaining of the information or the doing of such other things in relation to it as may be prescribed.

Section 61 provides for the establishment of a Patient Information Advisory Group which is discussed in *Chapter 8*.

Freedom of Information Act 2000

The purpose of this Act is to provide a general right of access to information held by public authorities. However, personal information is regarded as exempt information and comes within the provisions of the Data Protection Act 1998. The two Acts work separately, so that applications for access to personal information must be made under the Data Protection Act 1998 (see section 40, Freedom of Information Act 2000). Under section 41 of the Freedom of Information Act 2000 information is exempt from the provisions of the Act if it was obtained by the public authority from any other person (including another public authority), and the disclosure of the information to the public (otherwise than under this Act) by the public authority holding it would constitute a breach of confidence actionable by that or any other person. The Information Commissioner appointed under the Freedom of Information Act also holds the role of Data Protection Commissioner. Other provisions of the Freedom of Information Act are brought into effect in 2004 instead of being gradually implemented over several years.

References

Department of Health (2000) Data Protection Act 1998: protection and use of patient information. HSC 2000/009. DoH, London

Gaskin v. *United Kingdom* (1989) 12 EHRR 36 (ECt HR)

Information Commissioner (Registrar), Wycliffe House, Water Lane, Wilmslow, Cheshire SK9 5AF. Information line: 01625 545745; switchboard: 01625 545700; Fax: 01625 524510

Information Commissioner Legal Guidance on Data Protection Act 1989, 2001. www.dataprotection.gov.uk (see above address of the Information Commissioner)

R. v. *Mid Glamorgan FHSA ex parte Martin* [1995] 1 WLR 110 CA

4

Confidentiality and the courts

Box 4.1: Breach of confidentiality

Arthur Green, a physiotherapist at Roger Park Hospital, had been told by a patient, Dan Davies, that his injuries occurred when he was attempting to burgle a house and fell from a window. Arthur promised Dan that he would never disclose this information. Arthur is then summoned as a witness for the prosecution of Dan who has pleaded not guilty to the offence. Arthur considers that Dan gave that information to Arthur because he trusted him and is reluctant to give evidence against Dan. What is the legal position?

Introduction

It is not always appreciated that there is no right or privilege for a nurse, doctor or other health professional to respect the confidentiality of information provided by the patient when required to answer questions by a court of law. Even a priest would be legally bound to disclose information learnt in the confessional if the judge considered that information given by the confessor was relevant to an issue arising in the court. This chapter looks at the extent and process by which the court can require a breach of the duty of confidentiality.

Criminal cases

If the police require information from potential witnesses in a criminal investigation, then the witnesses have to answer the reasonable questions of the police otherwise they would be guilty of a criminal offence. Where police wish to access personal health records then the provisions of the Police and Criminal Evidence Act 1984 apply. Under section 9, health records are excluded material and the police have to obtain permission from a circuit judge in accordance with the provisions of Schedule 1 to the Act. Many police forces have developed policies with their local accident and emergency departments over accessing patient information. It is important to ensure that these do not exceed the lawful powers of the police and respect the duty of confidentiality owed to the patient. The patient can give consent to the disclosure, saving the police having to go through the procedure under the Police and Criminal Evidence Act (see *Chapter 14*).

Court hearing

In the above case scenario, Arthur would have no right to refuse to give evidence in the prosecution of Dan Davies. A subpoena could be issued for him to attend court and give evidence. If he ignored this then a warrant could be issued for his arrest. If he obeyed the subpoena, but once in court refused to answer questions on the grounds that he would be breaching the confidentiality of the patient, the judge has the power to commit him to prison until he has 'purged his contempt'.

In retrospect, Arthur should never have made the promise to Dan. A health professional cannot promise a patient that certain information will be kept confidential whatever circumstances arise since the court can direct the disclosure of that information. It is preferable for the practitioner to make the patient aware before confidential information of a criminal nature might be disclosed that a guarantee of absolute secrecy cannot be given.

Exceptions to the judge's powers to require evidence to be given

Legal professional privilege

This covers confidential communications between clients and their legal advisers for the purpose of giving or receiving legal advice, and to any communications whose dominant purpose is the prosecution or defence of legal proceedings. The judge cannot order disclosure of such communications. The reason is that it is in the interests of justice for a client to be able to confide fully with legal advisers without fear that such communications would be ordered to be disclosed in court. Reports to legal advisers are also privileged from disclosure if the principal purpose for which they were written is in contemplation of litigation.

Sometimes there may be several purposes behind the preparation of a report, eg. following a health and safety accident, where the report can be used for both management purposes in order to prevent a similar accident arising again and for legal purposes. This was the situation in the case of *Waugh* v. *British Railway Board* [1980]. In this case, the House of Lords held that if the predominant purpose behind the report is for advice and use in litigation, then it will be privileged from disclosure. This ruling was applied in the case of *Lask* v. *Gloucester* [1985] (*Box 4.2*). In the Freedom of Information Act 2000 (see *Chapter 3*) the existence of legal professional privilege was recognised and supported. Section 42 of the Freedom of Information Act states that information in respect of which a claim to legal professional privilege or, in Scotland, to confidentiality of communications could be maintained in legal proceedings is exempt information.

Public interest immunity

The other exception to the right of the judge to order disclosure of any document relevant to an issue before it, is that of public interest immunity. This covers such interests as national security. The privilege from disclosure is given under the sworn affidavit of a minister and can be overruled by the judge. Public interest immunity was considered by the Scott inquiry which recommended that immunity certificates should not be issued in criminal proceedings, if the liberty of the subject was at stake.

Box 4.2: *Lask* v. *Gloucester* [1985]

The court applied the ruling in *Waugh* v. *British Rail Board* [1980] in the situation where the health authorities claimed legal professional privilege in respect of confidential reports completed following an accident. The court held that in spite of declarations by the health authorities and solicitors to this effect, the documents were not covered by legal professional privilege.

Civil proceedings

Disclosure to the patient before litigation commences

In civil proceedings there is statutory provision in the Supreme Court Act 1981 for information to be made available before litigation actually commences and this information can include the detailed health records of the patient. If a client is suing in relation to an incident during care by a health professional his/her records could be ordered to be disclosed to the legal advisers or professional advisers of the patient. This right enables a potential claimant to have early access to the records to ascertain if litigation is justifiable.

Also, it is possible for the patient to obtain access to the records whether held in computer or manual form under the Data Protection Act 1998. However, there is no absolute right to access the records, and access can be withheld if serious harm could be caused to the mental or physical health or condition of the applicant or another person or if a third person identified in the records has requested that access should be withheld. (This latter exception does not apply if the third person is a health professional involved in the patient's care.) Fear of possible litigation would not be grounds for preventing patient access to the records.

The Woolf Reforms which have aimed at speeding up the process of civil litigation have emphasised the need for information to be made available between the parties before litigation commences and the judge in his or her new role as case manager has considerable powers to order the disclosure of information between the parties in the interests of justice. A preaction protocol has been set out with which parties must comply and sanctions are available if the times and requirements in the protocol are not met.

Access by the third party

Under section 34 of the Supreme Court Act 1981 disclosure can be ordered against a person who is not likely to be a party to the case. A possible situation where it would apply is shown in *Box 4.3*.

Box 4.3: Disclosure ordered against an NHS trust

A former patient is involved in a road traffic accident and sues the driver of the vehicle which caused the accident. This driver wished to have access to information about the patient held by the trust relating to its care in order to determine the likely prognosis of the patient. If, for example, there was concern that the patient was unlikely to make a full recovery as a result of the road accident, but that he suffered from severe disabilities anyway, these existing disabilities could affect both liability of the driver and also the amount of compensation payable (quantum).

Confidentiality ordered by the courts

Where sensitive issues are involved, usually involving children and mentally incapable adults, the court has the power to order the press to refrain from mentioning the personal details of those involved in any case. In the case of the boys who were found guilty of killing James Bulger, while their names were disclosed early on in their trial, upon their release from custody, the judge granted blanket privacy on the grounds that 'they were seriously at risk of injury or death if their identities were disclosed' (Gibb, 2001). The extent of the injunction was subsequently reduced in scope because it was considered to be excessive in its range. The Attorney General succeeded in an action brought against a newspaper which breached the injunction by publishing the addresses of the boys.

Conclusion

In deciding whether disclosure of confidential information is appropriate there is, in a sense, a hierarchy of priorities. The needs of justice in courts of law, litigation and prosecutions come before the individual rights of a patient to have information kept confidential. Practitioners should be aware of this important exception to the duty of confidentiality. The exception is recognised by the UKCC and all other registration bodies. It is important that the individual practitioner should understand the extent and limitations of the courts and police to require disclosure.

References

Gibb F (2001) Bulger killers win promise of secret lives. *The Times*, 9 January 2001

Lask v. *Gloucester* The Times Law Report, 13 December 1985

Waugh v. *British Railway Board* [1980] AC 521

5

The notification of infectious diseases

Box 5.1: Case scenario

Jenny Rose was a paediatric community nurse who regularly visited a child with a chronic lung condition who was being nursed at home. On one visit she noticed that the child's mother appeared to be very pale and thin and was told that the mother had a severe gastric disorder with diarrhoea. From the description of the illness, Jenny thought that Jane might be suffering from typhoid. Jane worked as a cook in a restaurant, was unwilling to seek medical advice and intended going to work that night. Jenny was concerned that Jane could have a serious notifiable infectious disease and therefore be a danger to customers in the restaurant. Jane insisted that Jenny should keep the information confidential. Where does Jenny stand?

Introduction

There are very few statutes which require information to be given to the police or other public authorities, but public health and the control of infectious diseases is one major exception.

Notifiable diseases

Diseases which are notifiable are shown in *Table 5.1*.

Table 5.1: Notifiable diseases	
Category A	cholera, plague, relapsing fever, smallpox, typhus
Category B	acquired immune deficiency syndrome (AIDS), acute encephalitis, acute poliomyelitis, meningitis, meningo-coccal septicaemia, anthrax, diphtheria, dysentery, paratyphoid fever, typhoid fever, viral hepatitis, leprosy, leptospirosis, measles, mumps, rubella, whooping cough, malaria, tetanus, yellow fever, ophthalmia neonatorum, scarlet fever, tuberculosis, rabies and viral haemorrhagic fever

Category A covers those notifiable diseases which come under the duties set by the Public Health (Control of Disease) Act 1984. These diseases must be reported to the local authority. Those diseases under category B are covered by Regulation 3 of the Public Health (Infectious Diseases) Regulations, 1988 (SI 1988 No 1546) and the 1984 Act applies to a more limited extent.

Procedure of notification

Under section 11 of the 1984 Act a registered medical practitioner has a duty to notify the proper office of the local authority if he/she becomes aware, or suspects that a patient whom he/she is attending within the district of a local authority is suffering from a notifiable disease or from food poisoning. The duty does not apply if the practitioner believes, and has reasonable grounds for believing, that some other registered medical practitioner has complied with the duty.

What information must be notified? The information which must be given is shown in *Table 5.2*. The health authority must be notified within forty-eight hours of the local authority notification.

Table 5.2: Information which must be given (Public Health [Control of Disease] Act 1948, section 11

1. Name, age and sex of the patient and the address of the premises where the patient is;

2. the disease or, as the case may be, particulars of the poisoning from which the patient is, or is suspected to be, suffering and the date or approximate date of its onset; and

3. if the premises are a hospital, the day on which the patient was admitted, the address of the premises from which he came there and whether or not, in the opinion of the person giving the certificate, the disease or poisoning from which the patient is, or is suspected to be, suffering was contracted in hospital.

(NB. Section 11(4) imposes a criminal sanction on a person who fails to comply with an obligation imposed on him under the provisions set out above.)

Powers of the justice of the peace

Because of the importance of safeguarding the public health, justices of the peace (JPs) are given statutory powers to intervene. For example, under section 37 of the Public Health (Control of Disease) Act 1984, the JP has the power to remove a person to hospital if satisfied that the following factors are present:

- a person is suffering from a notifiable disease
- the sufferer's circumstances are such that proper precautions to prevent the spread of infection cannot be taken or that such precautions are not being taken, thereby causing the risk of infection to other persons
- accommodation is available in a suitable hospital.

Under section 38 the JP can order the detention of a person suffering from a notifiable disease in a hospital for infectious diseases. Other provisions for Public Health (Control of Disease) Act 1984 are set out in *Table 5.3*.

Table 5.3: Other provisions of Public Health legislation

Section 13 gives the Secretary of State power to make regulations to prevent the spread of notifiable disease and preventing dangers from the arrival or departure of aircraft or vessels

Section 43 enables the registered medical practitioner to take precautions in order to prevent the spread of infection where a person suffering from a notifiable disease dies in hospital

Section 44 requires the person in charge of the premises where a person with a notifiable disease has died to take precautions to prevent any one coming into contact with the body

Section 47 enables the Secretary of State to make regulations relating to the disposal of dead bodies

Section 48 allows the JP to make an order for the removal of a body and for burial within a specified time to prevent the lives of others being endangered

Venereal disease provisions

Venereal diseases are one of the few conditions, which have explicit statutory provisions covering confidentiality. The National Health Service (Venereal Diseases) Regulations 1974 place a duty on health authorities to ensure that any information capable of identifying an individual examined or treated for any sexually transmitted disease shall not be disclosed. The only exceptions to this duty of confidentiality are where the information must be communicated to a medical practitioner (or person employed under the direction of a medical practitioner) in connection with the treatment of persons suffering from such disease and for the purpose of such treatment or prevention.

The effect of this regulation is to impose extremely tight precautions against any unauthorised disclosure in genito-urinary clinics and treatment centres. Such clinics should not pass on any confidential information over the phone and should not even disclose information to the caller, unless there was clear evidence that the caller was the patient.

AIDS/HIV

Acquired immunodeficiency syndrome (AIDS)/human immuno-deficiency virus (HIV) was held to be a sexually transmitted disease for the purpose of the venereal disease regulations even though there are other ways in which the disease is transmitted [*X.* v. *Y.*, 1988]. The notification provisions of the Public Health (Control of Disease) Act 1984 do not apply to AIDS. Under the AIDS (Control) Act 1987 (as extended by the 1988 Act) reports are given to the Secretary of State on a number of persons who have tested positive to HIV.

Under the Public Health (Infectious Diseases) Regulations 1985, local authorities have been given the power to apply to a JP for the removal of an AIDS sufferer to hospital to be detained there. The JP is also given the power to make an order for a person believed to be suffering from AIDS to be medically examined. There are also powers in relation to the disposal of the body of an AIDS sufferer. Confidentiality in relation to AIDS/HIV is considered in *Chapter 6*.

Jenny's situation

It is pure chance that Jenny has come across a possible case of infectious disease. Jane is not her patient. Jenny only suspects that

Jane may have a notifiable and infectious disease; she does not know for sure. Since Jane works in the catering industry, if Jenny keeps quiet the public's health may be at risk. Ideally, Jenny should try and persuade Jane to seek medical advice but she could warn her that if Jane fails to take action then Jenny herself would ensure that Jane's GP or the local authority was notified. However, it should be made clear that Jenny does not have a statutory duty to notify the local authority of the possibility of the disease. If she were to pass on the information to the appropriate sources then she would have to rely upon the justification that the disclosure was in the interests of public safety. Disclosure in the public interest was discussed in *Chapter 2*. It is important that Jenny keeps clear comprehensive records of the reasons why she discloses any confidential information and to whom she makes the disclosure.

Reference

X. v. *Y.* [1988] 2 All ER 648

6

HIV/AIDS patients and the duty of confidentiality

Box 6.1: Case scenario

Staff Nurse Grey discovered that one of the junior doctors in the medical team was human immunodeficiency virus (HIV) positive. She felt that she was under a duty to disclose this information in order that the patients could be protected from cross-infections. Since her senior manager appeared to take little notice of the information, she informed the press. What is the law?

Introduction

The number of newly diagnosed cases of human immunodeficiency virus (HIV) infection rose to 2828 in 1998, the highest annual total to be recorded (MORI, 1999). The spread of infection across the country is still proceeding and recent research suggests that advice on safer sex is being ignored. A MORI poll for the Terence Higgins Trust (MORI, 1999) suggested that 56% of adults have not taken the disease into account before having casual sex. A campaign was launched by the Government at the end of 1998 to persuade mothers-to-be to have an HIV test. The prevalence of HIV among women giving birth in London has quadrupled since 1990 and only 30% of women who are HIV positive know that they are HIV positive (Murray, 1998).

A cure or vaccine has still not been discovered for acquired immunodeficiency syndrome (AIDS) and even though recent drug combinations have slowed the rate of the progress of the disease within the individual, it still remains one of the major scourges among the infectious diseases in the UK.

Laws relating to AIDS and HIV

This country has never passed an AIDS/HIV Discrimination Act. Although those infected may be subject to venereal disease legislation or specific notification provisions, there are no specific laws protecting the confidentiality of sufferers, or preventing discrimination in the workplace. Those who come within the definition of disabled for the purposes of the Disability Discrimination Act 1995 may have the protection of that Act and the regulations made under it. In general, AIDS/HIV victims have only the basic laws, including the rights under the European Convention on Human Rights, which apply to everyone, to protect them against unwarranted disclosure or unjustified discrimination.

There have been criminal convictions where an infected person has attempted to infect others. In Louisiana, USA, it was reported that a doctor who gave his lover the AIDS virus by injecting her with infected blood was given the maximum penalty of fifty years hard labour for attempted second-degree murder (*The Times*, 1999). In Missouri, a laboratory technician was convicted of stealing an HIV-tainted specimen and injecting it into his infant son to avoid paying child support (Bone, 1998). More recently in the UK, a man has been prosecuted for passing on to his girlfriend the HIV virus. Stephen Kelly was convicted of knowingly infecting a lover with HIV and was jailed for five years (Harris, 2001). He was prosecuted under the Scottish common law. It was announced by the Home Secretary that a new criminal offence of deliberately infecting a person with the HIV virus was to be created in England and Wales.

A nurse with AIDS and HIV

The UKCC has issued guidelines relating to the duty of any registered practitioners who find that they are suffering from AIDS/HIV to report the situation to their employer. This is a duty which could be subject to professional conduct committee proceedings if the practitioner failed to comply with this instruction. It does not follow that nurses would automatically lose their jobs, however, if there were a greater risk to patients as a result of the situation, employers would have to find the nurse alternative suitable work.

Other health practitioners

Registration bodies such as the General Medical Council and the General Dental Council recognise the necessity of an infected practitioner notifying the relevant officer at work, and ensuring patient safety.

Failure to notify

What happens when a healthcare professional appears to disobey the guidance of his/her professional registration body? Can anyone else take it upon him/herself to report that information?

A reported case

In the case of *X.* v. *Y.* [1988] the court ordered an injunction to be issued to prevent the disclosure by the press of the identity of doctors suffering from AIDS. The facts are shown in *Box 6.2*.

Box 6.2: *X.* v. *Y.* [1988]

Two general practitioners were diagnosed as having contracted AIDS. They received counselling in a local hospital, continuing with their medical practice. A journalist heard of the situation from an employee of the health authority and wrote an article for a national newspaper. The health authority sought an injunction to prevent any further disclosure of the information obtained from patients' records.

The judge granted the injunction on the grounds that the records of hospital patients, particularly those suffering from this appalling condition, should be as confidential as the courts can properly make them. He rejected the defendant's argument that it was in the public interest for the public to know the identity of these doctors.

The judge did not, however, agree to the health authority's application for the name of the employee who had disclosed the information to the journalist. The Contempt of Court Act 1981 enabled journalists to keep their sources of information secret subject to specified exceptions and the judge held that these exceptions did not apply in this situation. The journalist was therefore entitled to protect his source.

The outcome of the case was that the doctors obtained the injunction preventing newspapers publishing their names, but the hospital did not obtain an order for the name of the informant employee to be released by the journalists, even though that employee was guilty of a disciplinary offence and could have faced dismissal if he/she had been identified.

Justification for disclosure of AIDS and HIV status

Sims (1997) discussed the duty of confidentiality in relation to the question of whether a physiotherapist needs to know if a patient has HIV. Sims concludes that except when progression to AIDS has occurred (in which case the diagnosis will be known to the therapist), a physiotherapist does not need to know a patient's HIV status. The reasons he gives are:

- ❖ A patient's HIV status does not determine the choice or effectiveness of therapy.
- ❖ The adoption of universal precautions provides optimum protection against transmission of HIV and does not depend upon a knowledge of who is, or is not, seropositive.
- ❖ He also states that there is no reason why a patient should know of the therapist's status since the chance of contracting HIV from an infected physiotherapist is so remote as to represent virtually no risk.

Answering the question raised

In the case scenario Staff Nurse Grey should not have informed the press of the situation. She should have attempted to persuade her colleague to be open and honest with the employers by disclosing the situation to them. If the doctor failed to do this, then in a serious case, where danger to other colleagues and patients was feared, she could have notified the employers in writing of her concerns. However, she acted wrongly in going to the press.

Conclusions

The general principles which apply are:

- ❖ All registered practitioners have a professional duty to notify their employer of their AIDS/HIV status.
- ❖ Registered practitioners also have a duty to ensure that appropriate action is taken to ensure that patients are safe.

❖ This latter duty may require the disclosure of certain information to senior management or the appropriate person within the organisation.

❖ Any such disclosure should be made in complete confidence and be limited to the proper person.

References

Bone J (1998) Man injected his son with HIV to avoid payments. *The Times*, 7 December 1998

Harris G (2001) Five years for the reckless lover who passed on HIV. *The Times*, 17 March 2001

MORI (1999) Poll for the Terence Higgins Trust. *The Times*, 14 April 1999

Murray I (1998) Mothers-to-be are urged to have HIV test. *The Times*, 1 December 1998

Sims J (1997) Confidentiality and HIV status. *Physiotherapy* **83**(2): 90–6

The Times (1999) AIDS attacker jailed. *The Times*, 19 February 1999

X. v. *Y.* [1988] 2 All ER 648

7

Human fertilisation and embryology issues

Box 7.1: Case scenario

A woman who was having *in-vitro* fertilisation (IVF) treatment was involved in a road accident. Her sister, a nurse, who was with her at the time, knew that she was taking part in the IVF treatment and passed this information on to those caring for her in the accident and emergency department, who obtained from her IVF clinic details of the drugs that she was on. Subsequently, the patient complained that this information should not have been passed on. She did not want anyone else to know that she was receiving fertility treatment. What is the law?

Introduction

There are certain exceptional circumstances in which, although a general duty of confidentiality applies, the law reinforces it by specific statutory provision. One such example is human fertilisation and embryology. This chapter considers the law, the changes which have taken place and how it applies to practice (Morgan and Lee, 1990).

Human Fertilisation and Embryology Act 1990

Section 33 of the Human Fertilisation and Embryology Act 1990 restricts the disclosure of information relating to the register of individuals receiving treatment, services and any other information (which is held in confidence) that is obtained by any member or employee of the Human Fertilisation and Embryology Authority. Permitted disclosures include those shown in *Table 7.1*.

Further exceptions to disclosure include where a person wishes to defend an action or institute compensation proceedings brought under the Congenital Disabilities (Civil Liability) Act 1976. Section 34 of the 1990 Act permits disclosure in the interests of justice (*Box 7.2*).

In determining whether the interests of justice apply the court takes into account any representations of a person who may be affected by the disclosure, eg. the welfare of the child, if under eighteen years, and of any person under that age who may be affected by the disclosure. In civil cases the court can direct that the proceedings are held in camera (ie. in secret).

Table 7.1: Permitted disclosures under section 33(3) of the Human Fertilisation and Embryology Act 1990

a. to a person as a member or employee of the Human Fertilisation and Embyology Authority

b. to a person to whom a licence applies for the purposes of his functions as such

c. so that no individual to whom the information relates can be identified

d. in pursuance of an order of a court under section 34 or 35 of this Act

e. to the registrar general in pursuance of a request under section 32 of this Act (where it is questioned whether a man is or is not the father of a child)

f. in accordance with section 31 of this Act

Box 7.2: Section 34 of the Human Fertilisation and Embryology Act 1990, as amended by the 1992 Act: disclosure in the interests of justice

Where in any proceedings before a court the question whether a person is or is not the parent of a child by virtue of section 27 to 29 of this Act falls to be determined, the court may on the application of any party to the proceedings make an order requiring the Human Fertilisation and Embryology Authority to disclose information. This information is specified in section 34(2).

Offences

Section 41 of the 1990 Act makes it a criminal offence for any person to make a disclosure contrary to section 33 of the Act. Conviction could be followed by imprisonment of up to two years or a fine or both. The consent of the Director of Public Prosecution is required before criminal proceedings can be brought.

Disclosure with the consent of the person involved in the treatment

A permitted ground for disclosure under section 33(4)(b) is where there is consent by the person or persons whose confidence would otherwise be protected. Consent has to be given for specific purposes for disclosure to a specific person. Following the implementation of the 1990 Act, this was found to be too restrictive an exception to the duty of confidentiality. It would not, for example, have covered the disclosure by the clinic in the situation shown in *Box 7.1*.

The law was therefore amended by the Human Fertilisation and Embryology (Disclosure of Information) Act 1992 to widen the consent provisions and facilitate disclosure in exceptional circumstances. The amendments introduced by the 1992 Act are shown in *Table 7.2*.

The significance of the 1992 Act can be seen from the facts in the situation shown in the case scenario box. Under the 1990 Act the woman injured in the road accident would have had a right of action in respect of the disclosure. However, under the 1992 Act, if it can be shown that it was an emergency situation to prevent danger to the patient and it was not practicable to obtain her consent, then disclosure can be made.

Table 7.2: Amendments by the Human Fertilisation and Embryology (Disclosure of Information) Act 1992

a. the 1992 Act enables the patient to give consent to disclosure to a specified person and to give general consent to disclosure within a wider circle of people where disclosure is necessary in connection with medical treatment, clinical audit or accounts audit

b. before consent is given, reasonable steps must be taken to explain the implications of giving consent to the patient

c. disclosure of information is also permissible in an emergency where the person disclosing is satisfied that the disclosure is necessary to avert imminent danger to the health of the patient and at the time it is not reasonably practicable to obtain the patient's consent

d. the clinician can also disclose information to his legal adviser where necessary for the purposes preliminary to or in connection with legal proceedings

The 1992 Act also allows access to records of treatment to be given to personal representatives and those acting on behalf of the incapacitated patient in litigation

Children born as a result of treatment under the Act

There is a right of access to information for those who have been born as a result of treatment under the Act. Section 31 enables a person who has attained the age of eighteen years to access information kept on the register. An application to the Human Fertilisation and Embryology Authority under section 31 will result in information which shows that the individual has been born as a result of treatment services being made available. However, section 31(3)(b) stipulates that the applicant must be given a suitable opportunity to receive proper counselling about the implications of compliance with the request. The wording is interesting: the applicant does not have to have the counselling, merely the opportunity for it to be given.

Section 31(4) enables disclosure of information contained on the register to be made which shows that a person other than a parent of the applicant would or might be a parent of the applicant. However, there is express provision that the regulations cannot require the Human Fertilisation and Embryology Authority to give any information as to the identity of a person whose gametes have been used or from whom an embryo has been taken. The applicant can require the Authority to state whether the applicant, and a person specified in the request as a person whom the applicant proposes to marry, would or might be related.

Those under eighteen years

Those under eighteen years also have a right to ascertain whether they are born in consequence of treatment services and if they and their intended spouse are related. A suitable opportunity for counselling must be given.

Conclusions

The Human Fertilisation and Embryology Act 1990 and its amendments trace a careful path between preserving the confidentiality rights of those who have been in receipt of treatment services and the interests of children born from those services. The Human Fertilisation and Embryology Authority has prepared and regularly revised a code of practice to guide treatment centres in the implementation of the legislation and practice not covered by specific legislative provisions. At the time of writing there is pressure for those born as a result of artificial insemination by donor to have a right to know the identity of the donor. Any such right would require new legislation.

Reference

Morgan D, Lee RG (1990) *Human Fertilisation and Embryology Act 1990.* Blackstone Press, London

8

The role of the NHS trust and patient confidentiality

> **Box 8.1: Case scenario**
>
> Nurse Salmon worked in the gynaecology ward at a hospital and was known to gossip about her patients over lunch with colleagues. She did not usually mention their names. However, on one occasion, a well known television star was admitted to have a termination and in confidence Nurse Salmon told her friends about this, mentioning the person by name. If this comes to the notice of her employers, what action, if any, should they take?

Introduction

In *Chapter 1* the various sources of the duty of confidentiality were identified and it was noted that one of the sources was an implied term in the contract of employment. This term would require every employee who comes across confidential information in the course of employment to respect that confidentiality. Failure to do so could result in disciplinary proceedings, the ultimate sanction of which is dismissal. As an implied term, the employee may never have explicitly agreed to that term being included in the contract, but by operation of law when a contract of employment comes into being, the law would expect that certain terms would be implied to make business sense of that contract.

Such a term would be implied into the contract of every employee, not just those who, as registered practitioners, come under a professional code of conduct. Each employer, has a responsibility to enforce the duty of confidentiality across the organisation. Clear policies should be in existence for confidentiality to be respected. Sometimes employers might require an express term of confidentiality to be included in each contract of employment and registered practitioners might have an express duty to obey the professional standards of their registration body. Oral warnings, written warnings and, ultimately, dismissal should follow breaches of the duty of confidentiality.

In practice, as many practitioners would agree, hospitals, community health departments and GP surgeries are rife with gossip about patient information. The situation set out in the case scenario box is probably not atypical in that sensational information would rapidly spread across an organisation.

Nurses and other staff pass confidential information to colleagues when the justification for those colleagues having that information, ie. it is in the best interests of the care of the patient, is not present. Regretfully, it would probably be agreed that hospital staff are not in general good guardians of patient confidentiality.

Caldicott Committee

Concern about the need to improve the way in which the NHS managed patient confidentiality led to the appointment of a committee chaired by Dame Fiona Caldicott. Included in its recommendations (December, 1997) was the need to raise awareness of confidentiality requirements. It specifically recommended the establishment of a network of Caldicott 'guardians' of patient information throughout the NHS. Subsequently, a steering group was set up to oversee the implementation of the report's recommendations.

Following a consultation period the NHS Executive (NHS Exec) issued a circular on the establishment of Caldicott guardians (NHS Exec, 1999). The circular gives advice on the appointment of the guardians, the programme of work for the first year for improving the way each organisation handles confidential patient information and identifies the resources, training and other support for the guardians.

The guardian

Each health authority, special health authority, NHS trust and primary care group was required to appoint a Caldicott guardian no later than 31 March, 1999. Ideally, the guardian should be at board level, be a senior health professional and have responsibility for promoting clinical governance within the organisation. The name and address of the guardian is to be notified to the NHS Exec.[1] Action to be undertaken by each NHS organisation in support of the guardian is shown in *Table 8.1*. The guardian is expected to liaise closely with others involved in patient information such as information, management and technology security officers and data protection officers.

In making the appointment and defining the role of the guardian, the duties which are not to be delegated should be clarified. Guardians are responsible for agreeing and reviewing internal protocols governing the protection and use of patient-identifiable information by the staff of their organisation, and must be satisfied that these proposals address the requirements for national guidance/policy and law. The operation of these policies must also be monitored. Policies for inter-agency disclosure of patient information must also be agreed and reviewed, to facilitate cross-boundary working.

1   Miss Raj Kaur, NHS Executive, Confidentiality Issues, 3E58 Quarry House, Leeds LS2 7UE; Tel: 0113 2545000

Table 8.1: Action to be taken to support the guardian

Develop local protocols governing the disclosure of patient information to other organisations

Restrict access to patient information within each organisation by enforcing strict need-to-know principles

Regularly review and justify the uses of patient information

Improve organisational performance across a range of related areas: database design, staff induction, training, compliance with guidance, etc.

Resources/training/action

The preservation of the confidentiality of patient information is seen as a cornerstone of the NHS information strategy. The NHS Exec has advised that the modernisation funds which are being made available to support local implementation of the information strategy can be used to support Caldicott guardians. Seminars have been and are being organised within each region of the NHS, and persons interested are advised to make contact with the NHS Exec.[2] The NHS circular outlined the action which each organisation was required to take in the first year. The main activities are shown in *Table 8.2*.

Table 8.2: Specific tasks of Caldicott guardians in the first year

A management audit of existing procedures for protection and using patient-identifiable information leading to a report for the guardian to present to the senior management team as a 'stock-take'

The development of an improvement plan that will address any identified deficiencies

2   Bilal Hussain, Confidentiality Issues Section, NHS Executive Headquarters, Quarry House, Quarry Hill, Leeds LS2 7UE; Tel: 0113 2546383

Answering the question posed in the case scenario

One of the results of the implementation of the Caldicott recommendations and the establishment of guardians should be that the culture of confidentiality and sensitivity in handling patient information within NHS organisations should improve. Staff should appreciate that to disclose patient-identifiable information in unjustified circumstances is a serious disciplinary offence for which action will be taken by the employers. Nurse Salmon is clearly in breach of the implied term in her contract of employment, as well as being guilty of professional misconduct. She should face disciplinary proceedings as well as being reported to the UKCC (NMC after April 2002).

Guardians should aim to raise awareness of the need to protect confidentiality across the organisation so that each individual member of staff understands the seriousness of any breach of confidentiality. Disciplinary action is a sign to each individual member of staff (including doctors) that the duty of confidentiality is taken extremely seriously by the organisation. It is important, however, to remember that Caldicott guardians are only part of the programme to improve the way in which the NHS uses patient information.

Patient Information Advisory Group

Section 61 of the Health and Social Care Act 2001 provides for the establishment of a Patient Information Advisory Group. Regulations are to be drawn up by the Secretary of State to make provision for:

a. the persons or bodies who are to be represented by members of the Advisory Group,
b. the terms of appointment of members,
c. the proceedings of the Advisory Group, and

> d. the payment by the Secretary of State of such expenses
>   and allowances as he may determine.

Prior to the regulations under section 60 (*Chapter 3*) being placed before parliament, the Secretary of State is obliged to consult with the Advisory Group.

Staff concerns

Sometimes staff are concerned about safety and resource issues within an organisation and are faced with an apparent conflict between the need to make known serious deficiencies (ie. whistle-blowing) and the duty of confidentiality. It is to this apparent conflict that we look in the next chapter.

Reference

NHS Executive (1999) *Health Service Circular 1999/012. Caldicott Guardians.* NHS Executive, Department of Health, London

9

The law relating to whistle-blowing

Box 9.1: Case scenario

Alex Black, a staff nurse on an intensive care unit, was extremely concerned about the lack of adequate staffing levels on the unit. He had put his concerns in writing to his manager, but no action appeared to have been taken. On one weekend there was such a lack of staff that it was impossible to ensure that one nurse was attending every patient on a ventilator at all times. A young girl, injured in a road accident, was brought into the unit following surgery and was placed on a ventilator. Alex was asked to monitor her care as well as that of another patient being ventilated. The girl died and Alex considered that this might not have happened if there had been adequate staff levels. He knows that the family are ignorant of how low the standards of care were and is anxious that they should be notified. Would it be lawful for him to tell them?

Introduction

The last chapter discussed the role of the Caldicott guardians, together with the responsibility that each NHS organisation has to establish protocols for the protection of the confidentiality of patient-identifiable information. It is important that the duty of confidentiality is not used to stifle the raising of legitimate concerns about the functioning of the organisation and that staff have the opportunity to bring these concerns to the attention of management. Trusts have sometimes required staff to sign up to 'gagging' clauses in their contracts, preventing them from notifying external persons about their concerns.

Professional duty of staff to raise concerns

Practitioners registered with the UKCC have a professional responsibility to raise any concerns. Clauses 11, 12, and 13 of the *Code of Professional Conduct* (UKCC, 1992) all require the practitioner to report to an appropriate person or authority concerns relating to any circumstances in the environment of care, or where health and safety is at risk. Other registered practitioners also have Codes of Conduct which require them to raise concerns.

Protection under legislation

The Public Interest Disclosure Act 1998 provides statutory protection against victimisation for any employee who raises legitimate concerns with the employer. Protected disclosures are defined in section 1 of the Act and cover the situations listed in *Table 9.1*. The Act extends the rights under the Employment Rights Act 1996, which gives protection to employees not to suffer any detriment from the employer in health and safety cases.

The protected disclosures in *Table 9.1* are extensive and would cover most of the situations where a registered practitioner would have a professional duty to inform an appropriate person or authority under a code of professional conduct.

Table 9.1: Protected disclosures under the Public Interest Disclosure Act 1998
That a criminal offence has been, is being, or is likely to be committed
That a person has failed, is failing or is likely to fail to comply with any legal obligation to which he is subject
That a miscarriage of justice has occurred, is occurring, or is likely to occur
That the health or safety of any individual has been, is being, or is likely to be endangered
That the environment has been, is being, or is likely to be damaged
That information tending to show any matter falling within any of the above paragraphs has been, is being, or is likely to be deliberately concealed

How is the disclosure to be made?

Under the Act the disclosure is only protected if certain conditions are satisfied. The employee must have made the disclosure in good faith to his/her employer or other responsible person (S43C). Where the employee reasonably believes that a person other than the employer is to blame, then the disclosure can be made to that other person.

Disclosure is also protected if it is made in the course of obtaining legal advice (S43D) or, if the employer is a body whose members are appointed by a Minister of the Crown, the disclosure can be made to a Minister of the Crown (S43E). This would cover disclosures by employees working within the NHS. The Secretary of State has the power to specify other persons to whom disclosures can be made (S43F). Disclosures to other persons, (ie. those not included above), are protected if the conditions set out in *Table 9.2* and *Table 9.3* are satisfied (S43G). The conditions referred to in *Table 9.2* include the reasonable belief that the employee would be subjected to detriment by his/her employer if he/she makes the disclosure. Factors determining the reasonableness of the disclosure are listed in *Table 9.4*.

Special provisions apply where there is a disclosure of an exceptionally serious failure (S43H). Such a disclosure is protected if the employee:

- makes the disclosure in good faith
- reasonably believes the allegations to be true
- is not making the disclosure for personal gain.

And when:

- in all the circumstances it is reasonable to make the disclosure
- it is reasonable to make it to that particular person.

Gagging of an employee

The Act states that any provision in an agreement is void in so far as it purports to preclude an employee from making a protected disclosure. If a trust attempts to introduce a term in a contract of employment which prevents an employee making a disclosure which comes under the protection of the Act, that term is void.

Effect of the Act

Any employee who makes a disclosure defined as protected in the circumstances set out in the Act and who satisfies the specified conditions, is protected from suffering any detriment. Any dismissal or action short of dismissal could be challenged by application to an employment tribunal. Each NHS trust is required to draw up policies and procedures to implement the Act (HSC 1999/198).

Table 9.2: Conditions for protected disclosures under S43G

The employee makes the disclosure in good faith

He reasonably believes that the information disclosed, and any allegations contained in it, are substantially true

He does not make the disclosure for personal gain

Any of the conditions in subsection 2 are met (*Table 9.3*)

In all the circumstances of the case, it is reasonable for him to make the disclosure (*Table 9.4*)

Table 9.3: Conditions required under S43G

a. that at the time he makes the disclosure the worker reasonably believes that he will be subjected to a detriment by his employer if he makes a disclosure to this employer or another person under S43F

b. That he reasonably believes that it is likely that evidence relating to the relevant failure will be concealed or destroyed if he makes the disclosure to his employer

c. That he has previously made a disclosure of substantially the same information to his employer or a person specified under S43F

Table 9.4: Factors determining the reasonableness of disclosure under S43G

The identity of the person to whom it is made

The seriousness of the failure

Whether it is continuing or likely to occur in future

Whether the disclosure is made in breach of a duty of confidentiality

Previous disclosures to the employer or to another person prescribed by the Secretary of State

Compliance with any procedure specified for making disclosures

Procedures for bringing concerns to the attention of managers

Each NHS organisation should have established a procedure to ensure that it is possible for staff to alert senior management of failures within the organisation which could endanger health or safety or are of public concern. Any employee who has concerns which come within the provisions of *Table 9.1* should follow the procedure to ensure that senior management attention is given to these disclosures. The Report of the Bristol Inquiry emphasised the importance of establishing an openness within NHS organisations so that respect and honesty with patients is part of the philosophy of the organisation. (Bristol Royal Infirmary, 2001). In addition, the concept of clinical governance and the statutory duty under section 18 of the Health Act 1999 should ensure that trust boards are sensitive to the need to address concerns raised by staff. The Commission for Health Improvement as watchdog of standards within the NHS also has a role to play in ensuring that staff concerns about standards in the NHS are investigated.

Case scenario

Alex should ensure that his concerns are raised at a senior level within the organisation. He should not at this stage pass his views on to the family of the dead patient. If he receives no appropriate response from senior management and considers that a 'cover up' is taking place, he should be able to raise his concerns with higher levels of management, including the chief executive and the chairman of the trust. If they fail to respond appropriately, there may be justification for bringing his concerns to the attention of the Secretary of State.

There would be no justification for informing the press before he had exhausted all avenues within the NHS. Those charged with the clinical governance of NHS services should ensure that there are appropriate procedures for staff to make known their legitimate concerns. Staff should ensure that they utilise these procedures, acting in good faith but at the same time, as far as it is possible, protecting patient confidentiality.

References

Bristol Royal Infirmary (2001) *Learning from Bristol: the report of the public inquiry into children's heart surgery at the Bristol Royal Infirmary 1984–1995 Command Paper CM 5207 July 2001.* www.bristol-inquiry.org.uk/

Health Service Circular (1999) HSC 1999/198. *Public Disclosure Act 1998: Whistleblowing in the NHS.* Department of Health, London

United Kingdom Central Council for Nursing, Midwifery and Health Visiting (1992) *Code of Professional Conduct for the Nurse, Midwife and Health Visitor.* UKCC, London

10

Child care and the duty of confidentiality

Box 10.1: Case scenario

Jane told Angela White, a paediatric staff nurse, that she was being abused by her father, but did not want anyone to be told. Jane was fourteen years old, intelligent and mature for her age. What is the law?

Introduction

The scenario above illustrates several conflicting legal principles.

❖ The first is the duty of confidentiality in relation to information disclosed by a patient which can apply, in certain circumstances, to information disclosed by children.
❖ The second legal principle is the duty of care owed by the nurse to the child and the need to ensure that the child is protected.
❖ The third legal principle is the public interest in securing the conviction of a criminal since sexual relations with a girl under sixteen years of age is a criminal offence.

Duty of confidentiality towards a child

In the Gillick case (*Gillick* v. *West Norfolk and Wisbech Area Health Authority* [1986]), the House of Lords established the principle that a mature child who understood the significance of a proposed treatment could give a valid consent. Such a child has become known as a 'Gillick competent child'. However, while a 'Gillick competent child' can give consent to medical, surgical and dental treatment, and all associated diagnostic and anaesthetic procedures, a child (a child is a person under eighteen years) cannot refuse to give consent to life-saving treatment and the court would overrule any such refusal in the best interests of the child. The court overruled the refusal by a girl of sixteen to have life-saving treatment. The girl was suffering from anorexia and refused to have treatment (*Re W.* [1992]). More recently, the court ordered a fifteen-year-old girl to have a heart transplant (*Re M.* [1999]).

Similar principles apply in the duty of confidentiality to a child. If the child is 'Gillick competent' and confidentiality is in the best interests of the child, then the confidences of the child can be respected. Many paediatric nurses receive information from children which they do not pass on to the parents or guardians of the child.

Duty of care to the child

There would, however, be circumstances where the welfare of the child requires such confidences to be passed to the appropriate person. In the scenario here, Jane is said to be mature at fourteen years of age, but she is the victim of abuse. Jane's interests and protection require that the appropriate child protection agencies are made aware of this abuse in order that she can be made safe from the abuser and receive counselling.

The Children Act 1989 recognises as a basic principle of law the fact that the 'welfare of the child is the paramount consideration'.

This is the test which Staff Nurse White must apply to the situation. Does Jane's welfare require that notification of the abuse is passed on? The answer must surely be yes. Obviously, Staff Nurse White must make it clear to Jane that she cannot keep her confidences but should, for Jane's protection, ensure that the child protection agencies are notified. Staff Nurse White should also ensure that Jane obtains assistance and counselling. Even if the young person is over sixteen years and has requested that the information be kept secret, there may be circumstances, particularly where a younger sibling is at risk, which justify reporting the abuse to the appropriate person.

The application of the principle that the 'welfare of the child is the paramount consideration' requires a balancing act. On the one hand, the practitioner needs to take note of harm resulting from a suggested course of action; on the other hand, this needs to be assessed in the light of the benefits which arise. For example, a fifteen-year-old boy might disclose to a nurse that he stole from a shop. If this was an isolated incident the nurse might decide that it was not in the boy's best interests for the child protection agencies to be notified, thus respecting his confidence with suitable warnings against repetition. It is a question of judgement over what is the appropriate action and junior staff would probably wish to seek advice from senior staff. In one sense this would be a breach of confidentiality, but it would be justified in the interests of the patient since the nurse requires advice from a senior colleague on the appropriate action to take.

Child protection procedures

Professionals caring for children should be familiar with the local arrangements. They should know the procedure to be followed if abuse is suspected, the name of the reporting person, and how to access the child protection register.

A child protection register must be maintained by each local authority. It is designed to provide a record of all children in the area who are currently the subject of a child protection plan and to ensure that the plans are formally reviewed at least every six months. The register also provides a quick central point of inquiry for professional staff who are worried about a child and want to know whether he/she is the subject of a child protection plan. In addition, it provides statistical information about current trends in the area. Access to this register would be permitted to an agreed list of personnel, including senior medical staff or paediatric social workers in the local hospital departments.

The child healthcare practitioner should also be familiar with the child protection provisions of the Children Act 1989 and understand how an emergency protection order can be obtained, how it applies and the significance of a child assessment order (Dimond, 1996).

Duty to report a crime

There are very few specific circumstances in which the public has a duty to report a crime (see *Chapter 2*). However, where harm to children is suspected and there is a likelihood of continuing offences against children, the practitioner would have a duty to make this information known to the appropriate authority in the public interest. This is an exception to the duty of confidentiality and is recognised by most professional organisations. The UKCC recognises the duty of a UKCC practitioner to make such information known (UKCC, 1996).

Record keeping

When healthcare professionals disclose confidential information, the importance of record keeping cannot be exaggerated. It is essential that the practitioner records the reasons why confidential information was passed on and what exactly was disclosed. If there is a subsequent allegation of breach of confidentiality, then that recorded information should provide a defence for the practitioner.

For example, if a nurse has a reasonable suspicion that injuries being shown by a child were the result of non-accidental injury, he/she should record the nature of the injuries, and any other evidence suggesting abuse, along with the action taken. Butler (1994) has suggested a simple chart incorporating descriptions of type and extent of injuries and grades of mood/pain which can be used as a paediatric assessment sheet.

Conclusion

The issues of professional judgement which arise in relation to the confidentiality of information received from children are exacting. Assistance to registered practitioners, particularly health visitors and nursing staff can be obtained from the Caldicott guardian, the person appointed within NHS trusts to set standards and monitor the respect for patient confidentiality (see *Chapter 8*). It is important for a practitioner caring for children to support their personal development and growth towards autonomy and, where reasonable, respect their confidences. However, this must be balanced against the need to secure their welfare and best interests.

References

Butler K (1994) Nurse-aid management of children 1: accidents. *Br J Nurs* **3**(11): 579–82

Dimond B (1996) *The Legal Aspects of Child Healthcare*. Mosby, London

Gibb F (1999) Girl 15, is forced into heart op. *The Times*, 16 July 1999

Gillick v. *West Norfolk and Wisbech Area Health Authority* [1986] 1AC112

Re M. (Medical Treatment: consent) [19999] 2 FLR 1097

Re W. (a minor) (Medical Treatment) [1992] 4 All ER 627

UKCC (1996) *Guidelines for Professional Practice*. UKCC, London

11

Terminal illness and the duty of confidentiality

Introduction

The situation outlined in the *Box 11.1* is not unusual in health care, particularly in the care of elderly people and those suffering from terminal illness. Relatives are often informed before the patient, and they then ask health staff to keep this information from the patient because they believe that they are acting in the best interests of the patient: that the patient could not cope with the news, and that they will tell the patient when the 'time' comes. The 'time' is never clearly defined. Telling the relatives first is, of course, a reversal of what should be the legal situation.

The patient's right

The duty of confidentiality is owed to the patient. It is in theory the right of the patient to ask health professionals to keep information from the relatives. If the patient believes that he would prefer his wife and daughter not to know his diagnosis and prognosis, that is his legal right, even if this makes communication between relatives and staff difficult. However, when information is given first to the relatives and not to the patient, the relatives acquire power over that information which the law does not give to them. Their refusal to allow a competent adult patient to obtain necessary information has no legal basis.

European Convention on Human Rights

Article 8 of the European Convention on Human Rights recognises the right of respect for privacy. This right could be used as the basis of a legal action if a patient considered that there had been a breach of confidentiality. This is considered in *Chapter 1*.

Incompetent patients

There are only two exceptions to the principle that the patient should receive the information first: when the patient lacks the mental capacity to deal with that information; and when the information must be withheld in the best interests of the patient.

A person with severe learning disabilities, or an elderly person suffering from Alzheimer's disease may not have the capacity to take in information and make decisions on their own account. In such cases, the staff have to give information to the relatives. However, there is no legal right for the relatives to give or withhold consent to treatment on behalf of a mentally incapacitated adult. If an adult is incapable of making decisions for him/herself, the doctor must make the decision, in the best interests of the patient, taking into account the prognosis and what treatment should be given according to the reasonable standard of the profession (*F.* v. *West Berkshire Health Authority and another* [1989]). The doctor may, of course, seek the relatives' view on the proposed treatment, but the relatives cannot give or withhold consent.

If David in the above situation was held to be mentally incapacitated then it would be justifiable to tell his wife and daughter of the prognosis. Temporary incapacity following recovery from an operation would not count as sufficient incapacity to justify the relatives being informed first. If, after a few hours of recovery, it could be anticipated that David would recover his full faculties, giving information about the diagnosis should be delayed until he could be told and could decide for himself how he wished that information to be handled.

Severe harm to the physical or mental health of the patient

The other exception where information may lawfully be withheld is where hearing such news would cause serious harm to the mental or physical health of the patient. The Data Protection Act 1998 (Subject access modification) (Health) Order 2000 SI No 413 (see *Appendix II*) and the Access to Medical Reports Act 1988 (see *Chapter 3*) which permit access by patients to their health records and (certain) reports do not permit absolute access. They all recognise that where serious harm would be caused to the applicant then access can be withheld. The applicant can challenge such withholding of information and so clear reasons, based on the particular consequences to that patient as to why access cannot be given, should be known.

In other words, the withholding of information cannot be based on a blanket policy, eg. a policy such as 'in all cases of terminal illness the relatives must be told first'. Each patient must be individually assessed for his/her competence to deal with distressing information. It must not be assumed that simply because information is distressing it automatically would cause serious harm. A similar right of withholding information from patients has been recognised at common law by the House of Lords, where it was described as the therapeutic privilege of the doctor to withhold information in exceptional situations where consent to treatment was being sought (*Sidaway* v. *Bethlem Royal Hospital Governors* [1985]).

Relatives' annoyance

Many relatives may not know the legal situation and staff are often badgered by them for information which is properly the preserve of the patient. Relatives do not always wish to protect and promote the autonomy of the patient, and while healthcare professionals are moving away from more paternalistic attitudes in health care, relatives may still be wanting to shield the patient from distressing information and control the communication of such information.

Legal right of relatives to access patient records

In what circumstances, if at all, can relatives ask to see the records of a patient? Under the Data Protection Act 1998 the following persons have rights of access:

❖ The patient.
❖ A person authorised in writing to make the application on the patient's behalf.
❖ Where the patient is a child (a person under sixteen years), a person having parental responsibility for the child (the patient must either consent to the application or the patient must be incapable of understanding and the giving of access would be in his/her best interests).
❖ Where the patient is incapable of managing his/her own affairs, a person appointed by the court to manage his affairs.

❖ Where the patient has died, the personal representatives of the patient or any person who may have a claim arising out of the patient's death. (Access under this subsection can be prevented if the record includes a note, made at the patient's request, that he/she did not wish access to be given on such an application. Any information need not be disclosed, if it is not relevant to any claim which may arise from the patient's death.)

Even when the patient is mentally incapacitated there is no automatic right for a relative to access the records. The giving of patient information, as opposed to access to the records, has not in practice kept to such rigid lines and there will be many occasions when information is conveyed by ward staff to relatives on the basis that they are acting in the best interests of that mentally incompetent patient. There are considerable advantages if staff could sensitively learn from patients their views about information being given to relatives if the patient were to become mentally incapable. The patient's wishes could be recorded in the documentation. Information given with the consent of the patient is not a breach of confidentiality.

Conclusion

Staff Nurse Grey could justify her disclosure of information to the relatives if David is mentally incapacitated and the information needs to be given to the relatives in David's best interests, or if the information would be so distressing to David that it would cause serious harm to his physical or mental health. If, on the other hand, after recovery from the operation, David will become mentally competent, and if such information although distressing would not in fact cause serious harm, he should be told first. It may be David's wish that his wife and daughter are present when he is told, but then such disclosure to them is with his consent.

There may need to be a review of protocols and procedures for those wards and departments which have to communicate such information. Every care should be taken to protect the autonomy of patients, so that at this crucial moment in their lives they are not rendered powerless by the withholding from them of possibly the most momentous news they are likely to hear.

The Government's proposals on decision making on behalf of mentally incompetent adults were published in October 1999 (Lord Chancellor's Office, 1999) and at the time of writing legislation is awaited.

References

F. v. *West Berkshire Health Authority and another* [1989] 2 All ER 545

Lord Chancellor's Office (1999) *Making Decisions*. The Stationery Office, London www.open.gov.uk/lcd

Sidaway v. *Bethlem Royal Hospital Governors* [1985] 1 All ER 643

12

The problems posed by suicide and euthanasia

Box 12.1: Case scenario

Jenny White, a hospice nurse, is caring for Peggy who is in the terminal stages of motor neurone disease. Peggy lives at home and is cared for by her husband John with support from the community health team and social services. John confides to Jenny that he has promised his wife that when her suffering becomes unbearable he will help her to end her life. Afterwards, John says he will have no further desire to continue life alone. Should Jenny respect the confidential nature of this information?

Introduction

Health professionals who care for patients in distressing situations can become party to many intimate intentions. With those who are terminally ill, the perspectives of both carers and patients can become distorted in the desperate reality of the situation. The difficulty is in empathising with the patient and the relatives while retaining professional detachment in order to provide support and specialist experience. Practitioners must understand the legal implications of the situation so that they are not unwittingly led into criminal activity.

Euthanasia

The UK does not recognise a law permitting euthanasia, whether active or passive, voluntary or involuntary. To take any action to shorten a patient's life deliberately is to commit a crime. Jenny should be aware that John has told her that he intends to commit a crime, ie. killing his wife. Even though this may be in accordance with Peggy's wishes, to aid and abet the suicide of another is a criminal offence. As a result of the Suicide Act 1961, it is no longer a criminal offence to attempt to commit suicide. However, it remains an offence to assist another person to commit suicide.

If John were to assist his wife to die, he could be prosecuted. If he were to be convicted of murder there would be an automatic sentence of life imprisonment, the mandatory sentence for murder. If he were to be convicted of manslaughter the judge has considerable discretion in sentencing. Dr Nigel Cox (*R.* v. *Cox* [1992]), who prescribed and administered potassium chloride to a patient who was terminally ill, was given a suspended prison sentence following his conviction for attempted murder. In cases of compassionate killing, relatives in John's situation have been conditionally discharged or given probation.

In a recent case (*R.* (Pretty) v. *Director of Public Prosecutions* [2001]) (see *Chapters 2* and *3*), Mrs Pretty who was in the terminal stages of motor neurone disease applied to the High Court for a declaration that, if her husband were to end her life to save her from the suffering and indignity she would otherwise have to endure, he would not be prosecuted under the Suicide Act or other laws. She argued that it was her right under Articles 2, 3, 8, 9 and 14 of the European Convention of Human Rights to die with dignity. The High Court held that the Director of Public Prosecutions did not have the power to give an undertaking not to prosecute a person for the offence of aiding and abetting the suicide of another. The High Court held that the right to life and to dignity did not protect the right to procure one's own death or confer a right to die. She lost her appeal to the House of Lords which held that there was no conflict between the Suicide Act 1961 and the Articles of the European Convention of Human Rights. The House of Lords also held that any change in the law to permit voluntary euthanasia would require Parliamentary approval.

Letting somebody die

The law has been criticised by philosophers on the grounds that it would be more humane to facilitate a speedy death, than to let nature take its course (Dimond, 1996). In the Tony Bland case, the House of Lords had to determine whether it was lawful to end artificial feeding for a person in a persistent vegetative state. Tony Bland had not recovered consciousness since his injuries in the Hillsborough disaster. The dilemma of the situation was recognised by Lord Browne-Wilkinson:

How can it be lawful to allow a patient to die slowly, though painlessly, over a period of weeks from lack of food but unlawful to produce his immediate death by a lethal injection... it is undoubtedly the law and nothing I have said casts doubt on the proposition that the doing of a positive act with the intention of ending life is and remains murder.
(*Airdale NHS Trust* v. *Bland House of Lords* [1993])

In Tony Bland's situation, the House of Lords decided that there was no duty to keep him alive at all costs. Extraordinary treatments could be withheld.

The law distinguishes between a situation where there is no longer a duty in law to keep a person alive at all costs and allowing the patient to die, and a situation where action is taken to end the person's life. The former is not criminally wrong; the latter is. Letting Tony Bland die was not a criminal act because ceasing artificial feeding was held to be lawful because there was no duty to keep the patient alive at all costs.

The law also distinguishes between lawful acts such as those designed to reduce pain, which may indirectly reduce the length of life, and unlawful acts such as deliberately giving a patient a drug to speed death. Dr Bodkin Adams was found not guilty of causing the death of a resident in an Eastbourne nursing home when he prescribed morphine for her care. The judge, Mr Justice Patrick Devlin, directed the jury that although a doctor cannot deliberately end a life, the treatment given in this case was designed to promote comfort. Life was incidentally shortened and there were no grounds for a murder conviction (Bedford, 1961). This ruling still applies today.

Summary of the legal principles

If John were to bring Peggy's life to an end, even though Peggy gave her consent, John would be guilty of an offence. If he were then to attempt suicide, and failed, he could not be prosecuted for the attempt on his life.

Confidentiality

Jenny has a duty of confidentiality to Peggy and John and it is only if one of the recognised exceptions to this duty arises that Jenny would be justified in passing on the information.

John's intention to end Peggy's life

Despite the circumstances this is a criminal act. However, the law does not require a practitioner to inform the police of every crime they come across. There are statutes requiring disclosure of information but they are unusual. For example, the Road Traffic Act 1988 requires notification if there is a road accident leading to personal injury and the Prevention of Terrorism Acts requires notification of any terrorist activities. The UKCC recognises that there may be an exception to the duty of confidentiality where it is in the public interest for confidential information to be disclosed (see *Chapter 2*).

It could be argued that what happens between John and Peggy is a private matter; if they decide upon a suicide pact, that is their concern. However, the problems which John and Peggy are confronting are of considerable public significance. Society has a role to support those who find themselves in this situation. Could more be done to support Peggy in order that John does not feel that he has to end her life? Should Jenny be assisting the couple by bringing in expert counselling, improved pain relief, speech therapy (to assist in any dysphagia problems) and other specialist help?

John's intention to end his life

While suicide is not a crime, similar issues are raised in relation to John's feeling that he does not want to survive Peggy's death as are raised by her terminal condition. Support should be available to John to show him that there could be a future for him after Peggy's death, eg. counselling and assistance from those who have suffered in similar circumstances.

Conclusion

This is a difficult area of law since there is no clear statute or case law covering the duty of confidentiality and the exceptions to it, in circumstances such as these. The basic principles have to be identified and then applied to the particular facts.

One way of arriving at an answer to Jenny's legal situation is to imagine that she respected the confidentiality of John's intention, and that John ended Peggy's life but failed in an attempt to end his own.

John could then be prosecuted for causing Peggy's death. If it were proved that Jenny had been aware of the situation and failed to take action, she would put herself at risk of being found guilty of professional misconduct in failing to notify the appropriate persons and in failing to secure more help and support for Peggy and John. The UKCC requires every practitioner to act, at all times, in such a manner as to safeguard the interests of individual patients and clients. Jenny could even risk being accused of involvement in the actual killing if she were aware of John's plan and failed to take action, since her actions may be construed as amounting to aiding and abetting the suicide.

The solution must favour Jenny passing information on to the appropriate colleagues in order to secure support for the couple. Ideally, she should discuss her concerns with John and Peggy, if Peggy is mentally capable of being involved, and obtain John's consent to the confidential information being made known. In this way there would be no breach of confidentiality, since the person's consent to the disclosure would be a complete defence to any action relating to the disclosure. The importance of Jenny's record keeping in this dilemma cannot be emphasised enough.

References

Airedale NHS Trust v. *Bland House of Lords* [1993] 1 All ER 821

Bedford S (1961) *The Best We Can Do*. Penguin, London

Dimond B (1996) The right to die, euthanasia and advanced directives. In: Greaves D, Upton H, eds. *Philosophical Problems in Health Care*. Avebury, Aldershot: 51–65

R. v. *Cox* [1992] *The Times*, 22 September 1992

R. (Pretty) v. *Director of Public Prosecutions, Secretary of State for the Home Department Intervening.* Times Law Report, 5 December 2001 HL

13

The rights of transplant recipients and donors

Box 13.1: Case scenario

Staff Nurse Fawn works on a transplant unit and is approached by a journalist who is seeking to write a report on a recent transplant success. Nurse Fawn knows that the recipient patient is happy to be interviewed, but the journalist wants her to find out the name and address of the donor family, so that the public can have both sides of the story.

Transplant surgery is one of the medical miracles of the last decade and is clearly highly newsworthy. Almost every day there are news items about amazing transplant successes: sometimes generous relatives are reported as donating a kidney or part of a liver or even part of a lung; sometimes strangers have benefited from the final act of a dying person who was carrying a donor card; and sometimes relatives who, struggling to come to terms with bereavement, have still been prepared to agree to organ donation. Such situations give rise to very special issues relating to confidentiality. This chapter explores the legal situation.

The transplant situation: Two different perspectives

Where organs are donated after death to unrelated persons, two different families are linked in very different circumstances. The donor family is grieving, often after a very sudden death, frequently of a young person. The shock, the sadness, the feelings of waste and futility dominate their thoughts. The possibility of ever adjusting to that loss, and carrying on with ordinary life, must seem inconceivable. Into this context comes the request for organs to be donated. Where the deceased has always made clear his/her wishes to be a donor and carried a card, the law merely requires the relatives to confirm that they are not aware that the deceased had changed his/her mind. Where the deceased had not expressed his/her views and does not carry a card then the relatives are required to give consent. If organ donation takes place, the family and their friends still have to cope with the bereavement and the added worry that the transplant may fail and they could face a sense of a second loss and bereavement.

On the other hand, the recipient patient and his/her family have, for a considerable length of time, had to face the imminent possibility of death. They have been told that only a transplant can save the patient's life. The patient may have been placed on a waiting list for many months or even years. Then suddenly the call comes: organs are available and the patient is rushed to the hospital for preoperative checks in order for the transplant to take place. Patient and relatives are, of course, nervous, but there is an anticipation that at last there is a chance of life; they are looking to the future with hope, joy and happiness. One family is looking at the past, and the other at the future.

The general principles

The basic principles of confidentiality apply to the two situations. Both families are entitled to have the donation and the transplant kept confidential. If the recipient patient consents to information being given to the press, then this is without prejudice to the right of the donor family to remain completely anonymous and their address and details kept secret and vice versa.

It would be rare for any of the exceptions to the duty of confidentiality discussed in this book to apply in this situation.

However, disclosure as a result of the order of the court (*Chapter 4*) (eg. if litigation was brought by the recipient or his/her family alleging breach of the duty of care by the surgeon or even the donor's family) or in the public interest (*Chapter 2*) (eg. if an infectious disease had been passed on (*Chapter 5*) may, in exceptional circumstances, be justified.

The official policy

Transplant co-ordinators, who link professionals in the hospital at which the donor is being cared for with the professionals at the hospital at which the transplant will take place, work under very clear guidance. It is the official policy that the instructions of the donor family should be taken in relation to subsequent communication. If the family has requested anonymity and has also stated that they do not wish to receive any contact or communication from the recipient, then those wishes must be respected. Even if the recipient wishes a letter of thanks to be conveyed to the donor family, it will not be delivered if the donor family has expressed a wish for no contact.

All communications should be made via the transplant co-ordinators. Neither family should put their own name and address on communications. In this way, contact, where not prohibited, can be made through the co-ordinator, and the donor family can have information about the progress of the recipients. If either party subsequently want to make themselves known to the other, then this can be negotiated through the transplant co-ordinator. Transplant co-ordinators have a key role to play in sensitively passing on messages and facilitating the limited communication which is required.

What if the recipient fails to follow the rules?

Box 13.2: Case scenario

Polly, a sufferer from cystic fibrosis, had a heart–lung transplant and was told nothing about the donor and had no idea who he/she was, or where in the country he/she came from. On returning home from hospital, Polly wrote a letter of thanks to the donor family, sending it to the transplant co-ordinator at the hospital. Polly put her name and address on the letter. Although she had been told that this should not be done, she felt that it would be a poor letter of thanks if she was not prepared to put her name and address on the letter. Polly did not expect a reply because she knew it was the right of the family to request no contact. However, about a month later, she had a reply from the mother of the sixteen-year-old boy who had died in a road accident. As a consequence, correspondence between Polly and the donor family started and led to their meeting up. Fortunately, the donor family said that they benefited from the contact with Polly and the knowledge that their son's death was not in vain.

In the case scenario of *Box 13.2*, the donor family were able to handle the different situation of their family compared with Polly's family, but things may have turned out differently with considerable stress for both families resulting from the contact. For this reason, the official policy is in favour of anonymity of both parties.

Answering the question posed

In the case scenario (*Box 13.1*) Staff Nurse Fawn should refer the journalist to the transplant co-ordinator. She should give no information out about the recipient patient, even though the patient is consenting to the disclosure of the information. It is preferable for the transplant co-ordinator to have the responsibility for any communication with the press and, where the families are willing to be made known, for the transplant co-ordinator to work with the press office of the trust to channel such information and protect the families from harassment.

14

Powers of the police and access to information

Box 14.1: Case scenario

Staff nurse Paula Rose was on duty in the accident and emergency (A & E) department early one Sunday morning when a police constable came in asking for details of any patient who had been brought in and for whom there was evidence of a fall from height. The constable explained that a girl had been assaulted and raped while in her bedroom by an assailant who came in through the window. Her screams brought help, but he made his escape from the window and she believed that he had fallen and may have suffered fractures or bruises.

Introduction

A powerful reciprocal relationship often develops between accident and emergency (A & E) staff and the local police. The latter are at hand to arrest and tackle those who are violent towards A & E staff, especially at the weekends when alcohol is a factor. In turn, the A & E staff may feel under pressure to provide confidential information to police to assist them in making arrests and bringing charges against those who are guilty of violence.

Before the attempt to commit suicide was decriminalised under the Suicide Act 1961, police would attempt to obtain details of those who had failed to kill themselves in order that a prosecution could be brought. There are dangers in this reciprocal relationship between A & E staff and the police, since the duty of confidentiality owed by the practitioner to his/her patients may be broken without justification.

This chapter deals with what healthcare professionals are legally obliged to tell the police and when the police can request sight of medical records and obtain blood or urine samples.

Police and Criminal Evidence Act 1984

The police have no general powers to compel hospital staff to produce any information which they consider is relevant to their purpose. The healthcare professional's duty of confidentiality is respected but the Police and Criminal Evidence Act 1984 (PACE 1984) (Kennedy and Grubb, 1994) sets out a procedure for personal health information that can be accessed by the police. Police do not have a right to search and access personal records unless special provisions are complied with. Personal records include records relating to an individual (whether living or dead) which could identify that individual and/or relate to his/her physical or mental health or to his/her (spiritual) counselling or assistance. Access to personal records can be obtained if the special procedure set out in Schedule 1 to PACE 1984 is followed. It covers information which is acquired in the course of a trade, business or profession and which is held subject to an express or implied term that it should be held in confidence.

Human tissue or tissue fluid, which has been taken for the purposes of diagnosis or medical treatment, is excluded material and must be held in confidence by all staff. Police have to have specific powers and follow the special procedure if they want access to excluded material.

Special procedure for access

A constable can apply to a circuit judge and if the latter is satisfied that one or other of two sets of access conditions is fulfilled (*Tables 14.1* and *14.2*), then the judge can make an order requiring a person who appears to be in possession of the material to produce it. The constable must then have access to the material not later than seven days from the date of the order or any other specified period.

If the possessor of the material fails to comply with the order and produce the information or permit access to it, then the judge, if he/she is satisfied that the access conditions exist and the order has not been complied with, can issue a warrant authorising the constable to enter and search the premises. The judge can also deal with the offender as if he/she were in contempt of court.

Table 14.1: First set of access conditions

The first set of access conditions apply if there are reasonable grounds for believing that:

- a serious arrestable offence has been committed
- there is special procedure material, but not excluded material
- the material is likely to be of substantial value in the investigation
- the material is likely to be relevant evidence
- other methods of obtaining the material have been tried without success
- it is in the public interest that the material should be produced or that access should be given.

Table 14.2: Second set of access conditions

a. there are reasonable grounds for believing that there is material which consists of or includes excluded material or special procedures on the premises

b. but for section 9(2) a search could have been authorised...

c. the issue of a warrant would have been appropriate

Voluntary disclosure of confidential information

Many health organisations would not wait for an order from a circuit judge before making information available to the police. Where it is clear that a health organisation has information that is relevant to a police investigation, and for which disclosure is justified in the public interest (on the grounds that it involves a serious threat to the health and safety of an individual) then this limited information can be made available voluntarily (*R.* v. *Singleton* [1994]). For example, if the police are able to give a detailed description of the person wanted in connection with a serious arrestable offence and that person has received treatment in the A & E department, then that information could be given to the police.

However, the police would not be permitted to look through the records of all persons treated that day in the hope that they might identify a possible suspect. If there is doubt over the category that any particular set of records comes into, then it would probably be wiser to refuse disclosure. The Department of Health (DoH) has advised that disclosure of confidential information to the police in serious criminal cases such as murder, manslaughter and rape would be justified (DoH, 1996). The British Medical Association (BMA) has prepared guidance on disclosing confidential information to the police (BMA, 1988).

Many A & E departments have arrangements which circumvent the necessity of the police obtaining an order from a circuit judge. These arrangements recognise the duty of confidentiality of the staff and the narrow exception of disclosure in the public interest. These local arrangements should be recorded in a procedure which guides both police and A & E staff. The procedure should contain details of the resolution of any disputes between A & E departments and the police.

Healthcare professionals as witnesses

If the police are investigating a crime and ask questions of a healthcare professional as part of that investigation, then the practitioner would be obliged to answer honestly and fully any questions put to him/her. The fact that some of the information relates to confidential patient material may provide a lawful excuse, and therefore defence, for not answering those questions (*Rice* v. *Connolly* [1966]). As a potential witness he/she would be expected to provide a statement to the police. In such circumstances, it would be advisable for the practitioner to obtain the assistance of a senior manager or lawyer to the health organisation before making the statement, especially if confidential information were required.

Where questions are asked in court, the practitioner is unable to rely upon any justification for not disclosing information on the grounds that it was confidential (see *Chapter 4*).

Road traffic offences and the Prevention of Terrorism Act 1988–2000

These statutes involve a duty to provide information to the police. Following a road accident which has led to personal injuries it would be a criminal offence for a health professional to refuse to notify the police of the name and address of those involved in the accident (*Hunter* v. *Mann* [1974]).

Similarly, any person finding evidence of terrorist activity (eg. the location of weapons) has a clear duty to report this to the police. Failure to do so is a criminal offence.

Intimate samples

Section 65 of PACE 1984 defines an intimate sample as: 'A sample of blood, semen, or any other tissue fluid, urine, saliva or pubic hair, or a swab taken from a person's body orifice.' The taking of intimate samples by the police is covered under section 62 of PACE 1984. This enables an intimate sample to be taken from a person in police detention if the police officer of at least superintendent rank authorises it to be taken and the appropriate consent has been given. It can only be authorised if the conditions set out in *Table 14.3* are satisfied.

Table 14.3: Conditions for authorising the taking of intimate samples
Such authorisation is given if there are reasonable grounds:
• for suspecting the involvement of the person from whom the sample is to be taken in a serious arrestable offence
• for believing the sample will tend to confirm or disprove his/her involvement.

The authorisation can be given orally, but must be confirmed in writing. The consent of the person in detention must be given in writing and he/she must be told of the authorisation and the grounds for giving it, including the nature of the offence of which he/she is suspected. All this information must be recorded by the police. Apart from urine and saliva, an intimate sample can only be taken by a registered medical practitioner.

It should be noted that consent in writing is an express requirement of the legality of taking any intimate samples. In some circumstances it can be an offence not to provide a sample; under road traffic legislation it is an offence to refuse to supply a sample of breath, blood or urine in drink driving cases. In other cases, refusal to provide a sample can lead to an inference of guilt.

Non-intimate samples

Non-intimate samples (*Table 14.4*) can be taken without consent under section 63(3) of PACE 1984 if the person is in police detention or held in police custody and an officer of at least the rank of superintendent authorises it to be taken.

Table 14.4: Definition of a non-intimate sample
Sample of hair other than pubic hair
Sample taken from a nail or from under a nail
Swab taken from any part of a person's body other than a body orifice
A footprint or a similar impression of any part of a person's body other than part of his/her hand

Involvement of health professionals in taking samples

If the patient refused to provide an intimate sample, it would be unlawful for a health professional to give to the police a sample which had been taken for other purposes, eg. diagnosis.

Case scenario

Paula should be able to refer to a local procedure regarding her duty to supply information to the police. It is likely that this procedure would state that the prior approval of the consultant in charge of the A & E department should be obtained before the disclosure of confidential information to the police.

In these specific circumstances, if the police had a fairly full description of the assailant, then the consultant might be justified in disclosing to the police the fact that a man meeting that description has been treated in the A & E department and pass on to the police details of that person's name and address. Handing the police the record of all people treated in the A & E department that day or the previous night would not be justified.

Conclusion

Health professionals have to walk a tightrope between the public interest in securing health and safety and the rights of the patient to have information kept confidential. The advice given by the UKCC in its *Guidelines for Professional Practice* (UKCC, 1996) and the codes of practice of other health professionals should be followed and comprehensive records kept of the police visit and the action taken.

References

British Medical Association (1988) *Philosophy and Practice of Medical Ethics*. BMA, London

Department of Health (1996) *Protection and the Use of Patient Information*. HMSO, London

Hunter v. *Mann* [1974] QB 767

Kennedy I, Grubb A (1994) *Medical Law Text with Materials*. 2nd edn. Butterworth, London

R. v. *Singleton* The Times Law Report, 22 June 1944

Rice v. *Connolly* [1966] 2 All ER 649

United Kingdom Central Council for Nursing, Midwifery and Health Visiting (1996) *Guidelines for Professional Practice*. UKCC, London

15

Child protection and unsuitable employees

Box 15.1: Case scenario

Mavis Brown learnt that Bob Downs was applying for the post of care assistant to work in the paediatric ward. She knew him from her home town where he had a reputation as a child abuser. What action should she take?

Introduction

In *Chapter 10* it was established that the protection of a child is a significant exception to the duty of confidentiality. If the safety or health or welfare of the child is endangered then any person would be justified in the public interest in ensuring that appropriate action was taken to safeguard the interests of that child, even though this entailed a breach of the duty of confidentiality.

This chapter looks at the statutory provisions for checking on the suitability for people to work with children. The Department of Health (DoH) and other organisations have issued guidance on inter-agency co-operation (DoH *et al*, 1999). The chapter also discusses The Sexual Offenders Act 1997; its provisions and the extent to which people can access information contained on the Register. The Rehabilitation of Offenders Act 1974 does not apply to those who work in health services so previous offences would have to be disclosed when seeking employment as a care assistant.

The Protection of Children Act 1999

This Act has four purposes (*Table 15.1*). It also provides for an independent appeal system. The Act defines a 'childcare organisation' as being concerned with the provision of accommodation, social services, or health services to children, where the activities are regulated by legislation. The definition includes all local authority social services functions relating to children, all children's homes — whether local authority, private or independent — nursing homes accommodating children, registered child minders and some NHS trust services for children. Clearly, a NHS trust with paediatric services would come under the provisions of this legislation. The effect of the legislation is that such organisations have a statutory duty to vet prospective employees, paid or unpaid, for work involving contact with children.

Table 15.1: Purposes of the Protection of Children Act 1999

It makes statutory the Department of Health's consultancy service index list and it requires child care organisations to refer the names of individuals considered unsuitable to work with children for inclusion on the list

It provides rights of appeal against inclusion

It requires regulated childcare organisations to check the names of anyone they propose to employ in posts involving regular contact with children with the list and not to employ them if listed

It amends Part V of the Police Act 1997 to allow the Criminal Records Bureau to act as a central access point for criminal records information, List 99[1] and the new Department of Health list. In other words, the Criminal Records Bureau will act as a one-stop shop in the carrying out of checks

1   List 99 is a list held by the Department of Education and Employment of those considered unsuitable to work with children. It has always been a statutory list

What should Mavis do?

Mavis has a duty to her employers to ensure that the appropriate checks are made about Bob as a prospective employee. (They should have checked even without Mavis' prompting.) They would apply to the Criminal Records Bureau about whether Bob is listed on their criminal records, List 99 or the DoH list. If he is listed, then he cannot be employed by the organisation to work with children. It may well be that when investigations are made, Bob Downs is found not to be on any list of sexual offenders and there are no clear facts, just rumours, about his child abuse activities. What action should Mavis take? In the absence of any clear information about Bob's potential danger to children, Mavis would have little justification in reporting him to senior management. She may be able to check that the procedures recommended by the Clothier Report following the crimes of Beverly Allitt are in place, so that precautions are taken to prevent harm to patients from employees (Allitt Enquiry, 1994)

What are Bob's rights?

Bob has the right of appeal. An independent review tribunal will review the way in which the decisions by the DoH to place the individual on the list have been reached (ie. a review confined solely to procedure). It will also examine the evidence afresh and make its own decision on the merits of the particular case.

Data Protection Commissioner's checklist

The setting up of a Register which contains personal information about child protection could be a breach of data protection legislation unless specific principles are followed (DoH *et al*, 1999). These include the requirements that:

- ❖ There must be a legitimate purpose to hold the data, with a restriction on secondary use of the material.
- ❖ The information must be shared in order for that purpose to be fulfilled.
- ❖ The parties concerned have the legal power to disclose the personal information for that purpose.
- ❖ The extent of the information held is necessary for the purpose.
- ❖ Either the consent of the individual has been obtained or there is an overriding public interest or justification for disclosing the information.
- ❖ The disclosure comes under the exemptions recognised by the Data Protection Acts 1984 and 1998 (eg. prevention or detection of a crime).
- ❖ Compliance with other data protection principles is secured (see *Chapter 3*) covering the minimum amount of data necessary, the accuracy, the length of time it is retained, access by individuals, and its storage.

The Court of Appeal ruled that the list maintained by the DoH of people who were thought unsuitable to work with children was neither unlawful nor was it operated unreasonably (*R.* v. *Secretary of State for Health ex parte* C [2000]).

The Sexual Offenders Act 1997

The Sexual Offenders Act 1997 was passed in order to ensure that once a sex offender had served his sentence and was about to be released, he would still be subject to some form of supervision to protect persons against the risk of his reoffending. Part 1 of the Act requires the notification of information to the police by persons who have committed certain sexual offences.

Provisions of the Act

A summary of the provisions of Part 1 of the Act is as follows:

- sex offenders subject to notification requirements
- the effect of notification requirements
- offences committed
- young sex offenders
- certificates for the purposes of Part 1
- interpretation of Part 1.

Schedule 1 of the Act sets out the offences to which provisions of Part 1 apply. *Table 15.2* lists these offences set out in Part 1, but omits details of the relevant Act and section number of the offence. Individuals who have been convicted of any of these offences have a notification duty under the Act.

Others convicted of one of the offences shown in *Table 15.2* are also included by the Act if:

❖ They are still to be dealt with after a conviction or a finding of not guilty by reason of insanity.
❖ They are currently serving a sentence of imprisonment, or a time of service detention, or a community service order.
❖ They are subject to supervision, having served all or part of their sentence.
❖ They are detained in hospital or subject to a guardianship order after conviction.
❖ They are detained in hospital following a verdict of not guilty by reason of insanity or to be under a disability.

There are certain exceptions to the list in *Table 15.2* where the offender is under a specified age, depending upon the length of sentence.

Table 15.2: Persons subject to a notification requirement

A person conficted after 1 September 1997 of:

- rape
- intercourse with a girl under thirteen years
- intercourse with a girl between thirteen and sixteen
- incest by a man
- buggery
- indecency between men
- indecent assault on a woman
- indecent assault on a man
- assault with intent to commit buggery
- causing or encouraging prostitution of, intercourse with or indecent assault of girl under sixteen
- indecent conduct towards young children
- inciting girl under sixteen to have incestuous sexual intercourse
- indecent photograph of children

A person found not guilty of one of the offences listed above by reason of insanity, or to be under a disability and to have done the act charged against him in respect of such an offence

A person cautioned by a constable in respect of such an offence, which at the time when the caution is given, he has admitted

How long do the provisions of notification apply?

Section 1(4) sets out a table giving the time limits for the application of the notification provisions. These vary from an indefinite period (those sentenced to life imprisonment) or for a term of thirty months or more in respect of one of the specified offences to a minimum of a period of five years following the conviction or the finding. Those guilty of the most serious crimes will remain on the register till death Those sent to prison for six to thirty months will remain on the register for ten years. Section 1(5) and (6) cover the situation where a person is convicted of several offences to which Part 1 provisions apply.

What is required by the notification provisions?

A person who comes under the offence provisions set out in section 1 and Schedule 1 is required, before the end of the period of fourteen days beginning with the relevant date or, if later, the commencement of this part, to notify the police of the following information: his name, and, where he also uses one or more other names, each of those names; and his home address (S2(1)). In addition, under section 2(2) the person must notify the police of any change of his name or change of his home address, or any premises where he has resided for a qualifying period. The notification to the police must also include his date of birth, his name on the relevant date, and his home address on that date. Any time when the person is remanded or committed to custody by order of court, is serving a sentence of imprisonment, is detained in hospital, or is outside the UK, is disregarded in determining any relevant period of time.

How is notification made?

The individual can give notification by attending at a police station in his local police area and giving an oral notification to any police officer, or to any person authorised for the purpose by the officer in charge of the station. Alternatively, the individual can send a written notification to any such police station (S2(5)). The notification must be acknowledged in writing and the Secretary of State can direct the form of the acknowledgement.

Consequences of failing to comply with notification provisions

Any person under a duty to make a notification who fails to comply, without reasonable cause, is guilty of an offence. Likewise, a person who provides any information which he knows to be false (S3(1)).

Young offenders

Section 4 applies the provisions of Part 1 to those sentences being served by young offenders. The period during which notification is required is halved for those under eighteen years (S4(2)). Parents can be directed by the court to fulfil the notification provisions for certain offenders who are under eighteen years, until they become eighteen.

Home Office guidance

The Home Office issued guidance in 1997 (Home Office, 1997). This provides a summary of the Act, sources for additional information, format of the official acknowledgement form, notice of requirement to register, and certification of conviction or finding. Appendix A sets out interim guidance on the way in which police forces should manage the information they receive about sex offenders subject to the Act and the criteria which should govern those decisions. An annex to Appendix A summarises some of the cases relevant to police disclosure. Appendix B provides supplementary guidance on the new requirements, the cautioning of a sex offender, the statutory forms, and the treatment of mentally disordered offenders under the Act.

Implementation of the Act and confidentiality

The Sex Offenders Act 1997 came into force on 1 September 1997 (The Sex Offenders Act 1997 (Commencement Order) 1997 Statutory Instrument 1997, No 1920). There have been concerns over who had access to the Register kept by the police, eg. could neighbours be told when a sex offender moves into the area? The guidance issued by the Home Office (1997) cites a case (*R.* v. *Chief Constable of North Wales*

Police ex parte AB [1997]) (*Box 15.2*) where it was held that in certain circumstances disclosure about offenders by the police to third parties was justifiable, but blanket disclosure policies were objectionable and any decision to disclose must depend upon a careful consideration of the facts of the case.

However, any NHS trust officer who enquired of the Register about persons moving to the locality of a children's ward would probably come within the range of justifiable disclosure. The contents of the Register cannot be automatically made available to any interested persons: the police, who are its custodians, have to exercise discrimination about to whom specific entries are notified.

Box 15.2: R. v. *Chief Constable of North Wales Police ex parte AB* [1997]

Following their release from prison after serving long sentences for sexual offences against children, AB and CD, a married couple, moved to the North of England and later to a caravan site in North Wales. After receiving a report from Northumbrian police, the North Wales police asked them to move on before Easter, when a large number of children were expected to visit the caravan site. They refused and the police then showed the caravan site owner material about the couple which had appeared in the local press. The owner then asked the couple to leave which they did. The couple applied for judicial review of the action of the police.

It was held that where the police obtain information about a member of the public it should not be disclosed except for the purpose and to the degree necessary to fulfil their public duties. This principle did not arise from a duty of confidence owed to the police to a member of the public, but from a fundamental rule of good public administration. However, if the police, after careful consideration, determined that it was desirable or necessary in the public interest to disclose information to prevent crime or alert the public to a particular danger, it would be proper to make such limited disclosure as was necessary to achieve that purpose.

Care Standards Act 2000

Under Part VII of the Care Standards Act statutory provision is made for setting up a list of individuals who are considered unsuitable to work with vulnerable adults. There is to be a single list established for both England and Wales and it will operate in a similar way to the list established under the Protection of Children Act 1999.

Conclusions

This whole area is fraught with ethical problems. On the one hand there is a duty to ensure that the welfare of the child is the paramount consideration. On the other hand, individuals should not unjustly be prevented from working with children if the evidence does not support a prohibition. Their rights to freedom to work would be protected by the Human Rights Act 1998. In practice, it is likely that where there is reasonable doubt about threats presented by a particular employee, the protection of the child must prevail. There may be many who do not in fact present a risk yet are prevented from working with children, and whose appeals against inclusion on the lists fail. However, others, who do present a risk (eg. close family members) but are not suspected of it, can pose a threat to children. The lists are required to ensure that employers have sufficient information about prospective employees. It is essential that access to these lists is closely regulated and regularly reviewed.

References

HMSO (1994) *The Allitt Inquiry Chaired by Sir Cecil Clothier*. HMSO, London

Department of Health, Home Office, Department for Education and Employment, National Assembly for Wales (1999) *Working Together to Safeguard Children*. DoH, London

Home Office (1997) HOC 39/1997. Sex Offenders Act 1997. For copies and further information apply to Neil Clowes, Sentencing and Offences Unit, Home Office, London; 0171 273 3609

R. v. *Chief Constable of North Wales Police ex parte AB* [1997] *The Times*, 14 July 1997, Current Law 460 August 1997

R. v. *Secretary of State for Health ex parte C* [2000] The Times Law Report, 1 March 2000

Conclusions

This book has covered a wide range of situations and laws relating to confidentiality, but it cannot claim to have covered every conceivable situation which is likely to arise. It is hoped that sufficient information has been given about the basic principles and legislation so that the health professional can apply these to any specific situation which arises. Each individual practitioner should be aware of the professional advice contained in his/her code of professional conduct and ensure that they keep up-to-date with any changes in the law or professional guidance. Inevitably, there are many situations which are not black and white, where the practitioner has to use professional discretion to determine whether the duty of confidentiality should prevail over any demands for disclosure, or whether the situation comes within a legally recognised justification of exception to the duty of confidentiality. As in so many areas of professional practice, it is vital that the situation on which the decision is made and the justifications for that decision are carefully documented. The report of the Bristol Inquiry (Bristol Royal Infirmary, 2001) has urged that there should be respect and honesty at the heart of health care and that there should be a partnership between patient and health professional. There are now in place statutory measures to ensure that staff are supported. If there are concerns, staff have the protection of the Public Interest Disclosure Act (see *Chapter 9*) in making a justified disclosure. In every NHS organisation there should be a person at senior level clearly identified as the Caldicott guardian with responsibility for promoting confidentiality within the organisation. It remains, however, a matter of both the law and professional practice that each and every individual health professional is personally and professionally accountable for their actions, including their decisions in relation to patient confidentiality.

Reference

Bristol Royal Infirmary (2001) *Learning from Bristol: the report of the public inquiry into children's heart surgery at the Bristol Royal Infirmary 1984–1995 Command Paper CM 5207 July 2001*. www.bristol-inquiry.org.uk/

Further reading

Dimond BC (2001) *Legal Aspects of Nursing*. 3rd edn. Prentice Hall Inc, Harlow, Essex

Dimond BC (1999) *Patients' Rights, Responsibilities and the Nurse*. Quay Books division, Mark Allen Publishing Ltd, Salisbury, Wiltshire

Foster C, Peacock N (2000) *Clinical Confidentiality*. Monitor Press, Sudbury, Suffolk

Hendrick J (2000) *Law and Ethics in Nursing and Healthcare*. Stanley Thomas (Publishers) Ltd, Cheltenham

Kennedy I, Grubb A (2000) *Medical Law and Ethics*. 3rd edn. Butterworths, London

McHale J, Fox M, Murphy J (1997) *Health Law Text and Materials*. Sweet and Maxwell, London

McHale J, Tingle J (2001) *Law and Nursing*. 2nd edn. Butterworth Heinemann, Oxford

Maclean A (2001) *Briefcase of Medical Law*. Cavendish, London

Montgomery J (1997) *Health Care Law*. Oxford University Press, Oxford

Finch J, ed. (1994) *Speller's Law Relating to Hospitals*. J Chapman and Hall, London

Tingle J, Cribb A, eds (1995) *Nursing Law and Ethics*. Blackwell Science, Oxford

Young AP (1989) *Legal Problems in Nursing Practice*. 2nd edn. Harper and Rowe, New York

Appendix I

Department of Health Circular HSC 2000/009

Section B, Schedule 2, Data Protection Act 1998 — Conditions relevant for the purposes of the first principle: processing of any personal data

1. The data subject has given his consent to the processing

2. The processing is necessary —

(a) for the performance of a contract to which the data subject is a party, or

(b) for the taking of steps at the request of the data subject with a view to entering into a contract.

3. The processing is necessary for compliance with any legal obligation to which the data controller is subject, other than an obligation imposed by contract.

4. The processing is necessary to protect the vital interests of the data subject.

5. The processing is necessary —

(a) for the administration of justice

(b) for the exercise of any functions conferred on any person by or under any enactment

(c) for the exercise of any functions of the Crown, a Minister of the Crown or a government department

(d) for the exercise of any other functions of a public nature exercised in the public interest by any person.

6.(1) The processing is necessary for the purpose of legitimate interests pursued by the data controller or by the third party or parties to whom the data are disclosed, except where the processing is unwarranted in any particular case by reason of prejudice to the rights and freedoms or legitimate interests of the data subject.

(2) The Secretary of State may by order specify particular circumstances in which this condition is, or is not, to be taken to be satisfied.

Section C, Schedule 3, Data Protection Act 1998 — Conditions relevant for the purposes of the first principle: processing of sensitive personal data

1. The data subject has given his explicit consent to the processing of the personal data.

2(1). The processing is necessary for the purposes of exercising or performing any right or obligation which is conferred or imposed by law on the data controller in connection with employment.

(2) the Secretary of State may by order —

(a) exclude the application of sub-paragraph (1) in such cases as may be specified, or

(b) provide that, in such cases as may be specified, the condition in sub-paragraph (1) is not to be regarded as satisfied unless such further conditions as may be specified in the order are also satisfied.

3.1 The processing is necessary —

(a) in order to protect the vital interests of the data subject or another person, in a case where

(i)   consent cannot be given by or on behalf of the data subject, or,

(ii)   the data controller cannot reasonably be expected to obtain the consent of the data subject, or

(b)   in order to protect the vital interests of another person, in a case where consent by or on behalf of the data subject has been unreasonably withheld.

4.   The processing —

(a)   is carried out in the course of its legitimate activities by any body or association which

(i)   is not established or conducted for profit, and

(ii)   exists for political, philosophical, religious or trade-union purposes,

(b)   is carried out with appropriate safeguards for the rights and freedoms of data subjects

(c)   relates only to individuals who either are members of the body or association or have regular contact with it in connection with its purposes, and

(d)   does not involve disclosure of the personal data to a third party without the consent of the data subject.

5.   The information contained in the personal data has been made public as a result of steps deliberately taken by the data subject.

6.   The processing —

(a)   is necessary for the purpose of, or in connection with, any legal proceedings (including prospective legal proceedings),

(b)   is necessary for the purpose of obtaining legal advice, or

(c)   is otherwise necessary for the purposes of establishing, exercising or defending legal rights.

7.(1) The processing is necessary —

(a)   for the administration of justice,

(b)   for the exercise of any functions conferred on any person by or under an enactment, or

(c)   for the exercise of any functions of the Crown, a Minister of the Crown or a government department

(2)   The Secretary of State may by order —

(a)   exclude the application of sub-paragraph (1) in such cases as may be specified, or

(b)   provide that, in such cases as may be specified, the condition in sub-paragraph (1) is not to be regarded as satisfied unless such further conditions as may be specified in the order are also satisfied.

8.(1) The processing is necessary for medical purposes and is undertaken by —

(a)   a health professional, or

(b)   a person who in the circumstances owes a duty of confidentiality which is equivalent to that which would arise if that person were a health professional.

(2)   In this paragraph 'medical purposes' includes the purposes of preventative medicine, medical diagnosis, medical research, the provision of care and treatment and the management of healthcare services.

9.(1) The processing —

(a)   is of sensitive personal data consisting of information as to racial or ethnic origin,

(b)   is necessary for the purpose of identifying or keeping under review the existence or absence of equality of opportunity or treatment between persons of different racial or ethnic origins, with a view to enabling such equality to be promoted or maintained, and

(c)   is carried out with appropriate safeguards for the rights and freedoms of data subjects.

(2)   The Secretary of State may by order specify circumstances in which processing falling within sub-paragraph (1)(a) and (b) is, or is not, to be taken for the purposes of sub-paragraph (1)(c) to be carried out with the appropriate safeguards for the rights and freedoms of data subjects.

10.   The personal data are processed in circumstances specified in an order made by the Secretary of State for the purposes of this paragraph.

Appendix II

Department of Health Circular HSC 2000/009, Data Protection Act 1998: protection of patient information

Part 3 — Rights of access to personal data
Access Rights

1.   In general the Act gives data subjects rights to access personal data about themselves which is held in either computerised or manual form, whenever the record was compiled.

2.   The rights give an entitlement to:
- be informed whether personal data is processed (which includes being held or stored)
- a description of the data held, the purposes for which it is processed and to whom the data may be disclosed
- a copy of the information constituting the data
- information as to the source of the data.

2.1   Data subjects have access rights to all records irrespective of when they were created (whereas the Access to Health Records 1990 restricted access to records compiled after 1 November 1991).

3.   There are exemptions to these rights:

i)   a request can be refused if the data controller is not supplied with the fee (see below) and such information as he may reasonably require to satisfy himself as to the identity of the applicant and locate the information requested;

ii)   where information is processed solely for historical or scientific (including medical) research purposes, is not processed to support measures or decisions with respect to particular individuals nor in such a way as will or may cause substantial damage or distress to any data subject, and where the results will not be made available in a form from which individuals can be identified;

iii)   where disclosing the personal data would reveal information which relates to and identifies another person (for example that a relative had provided certain information) unless that person has consented to the disclosure or it is reasonable to comply with the request without that consent. The factors listed in section 7(6) should be considered in determining whether it would be reasonable in all the circumstances. These provisions do not apply where the person to be identified is a health professional who has either compiled or contributed to either the record or the care of the patient;

iv)   in the case of personal data consisting of information about the physical or mental health or condition of the data subject (ie. most information held by NHS bodies) the Data Protection (Subject Access Modification) (Health) Order 2000 provides exemptions from the subject access rights in two situations:

a)   where permitting access to the data would be likely to cause serious harm to the physical or mental health or condition of the data subject or any other person (which may include a health professional);

b)   where the request for access is made by another on behalf of the data subject, such as a parent for a child, access can be refused if the data subject had either provided the information in the expectation it would not be disclosed to the applicant or had indicated it should not be so disclosed, or if the data was obtained as a result of any examination or investigation to which the data subject consented on the basis that information would not be so disclosed.

4.   Before deciding whether the exemption in paragraph 3 iv (a) above applies, a data controller who is not a health professional must consult the health professional responsible for the clinical care of the data subject; or if there is more than one, the most suitable available health professional. If there is none, or the relevant data concern certain social security matters specified in Article 2(c)(ii) of the Order, a health professional with the necessary qualifications and experience to advise on the matters to which the information requested relates must be consulted.

Responding to access requests

5.   A request for access must be made in writing, and no reason need be given. Subject to any applicable exemption, the applicant must be given a copy of the information and, where the data is not readily intelligible, an explanation (eg. of abbreviations or medical terminology). Data controllers may not charge for the explanation, but can charge a fee for the application and copying charges.

5.1   Regulations on subject access fees have been agreed up until 24 October 2001 and are publicly available on the Home Office website at: http//www.homeoffice.gov.uk/ccpd/dpsafmsi.htm. The regulations provide that a maximum fee of £50 can be charged for access to health records for a transitional period running until 24 October 2001.

5.2   The data controller is entitled to satisfy itself that the applicant is either the data subject, or, if the applicant is applying on behalf of a data subject that the person has been authorised to do so.

5.3   The obligation to provide a copy may be waived where the data subject agrees otherwise or it is not possible to supply a copy of the material sought, or to do so would involve disproportionate effort (for example because papers have been destroyed, or are spread around the country).

5.4   However, the person may not wish to access their entire record and therefore NHS bodies may wish to confirm what material the applicant requires before processing the request which will both decrease the cost of copying for the applicant and unnecessary work by staff.

5.5   The Act does not provide an express right to directly inspect records, although it is permitted with the agreement of the data subject and data controller. It remains Department of Health policy that such requests should be accommodated subject to the exemptions listed in paragraph 3 above.

5.6   Requests for access should be responded to promptly, and no later than forty days after the request and fee (and any additional information as to the identity of the applicant or the location of the information reasonably required by the data controller) are received by the data controller. In exceptional circumstances if compliance is not possible within this period the applicant should be advised accordingly.

5.7   Where an access request has previously been complied with, the Act permits data controllers not to respond to a subsequent identical or similar request unless a reasonable interval has elapsed since the previous compliance. There is no definition of 'reasonable interval', but regard should be had to the nature of the data, how often it is altered and the reason for its processing. The reason for the request(s) may also be relevant.

Rights of rectification

6.   If the data subject believes that data recorded about them are inaccurate the person may apply to the court, for an order, or to the DPC for an enforcement notice, either of which may require that the inaccurate data, and any expression of opinion based on it, is rectified, blocked, erased or destroyed.

7.   However, where the data is inaccurate but accurately records information given by the data subject or another person the Court or the Commissioner may instead order that the record should be supplemented by a statement of the true facts as approved by the court/Commissioner.

Index of cases

Index of statutes

Index